Rewire Your Brain

2 Books in 1:

Master your Mindset for Success &

Habit Hack Your Way to Happiness

Table of Contents

How To Change Your Mindset in 30 Days

7 Hacks to Change Habits in 30 days

How To Change Your Mindset in 30 Days

Positive Thinking & Behaviour for Success

By Leon Lyons

MindsetMastership.com

About the Author

Leon Lyons is a senior coach at Mindset Mastership, a life coaching business based in London, England.

Mindset Mastership teaches clients how human behaviour really works. Through our teaching we have helped worldwide clients gain a better advantage, to develop themselves and achieve more from life.

For further details, see:
MindsetMastership.com

Introduction

The truth is, none of us can wake up and remarkably change our lives other than ourselves.

Studies have shown that 80% of our daily thoughts are negative self-talk. This means unfiltered thoughts enter our minds leaving us with harmful emotions. We must find better solutions in controlling negative mindsets to help us turn our lives around.

We use powerful mindset change methods such as CTFAR & the 5 R's: these approaches will reprogram the way you think – AND build a stronger, more positive mind.

The Seven-Step plan is easy, simple, clear and a little fun. The first few days we'll begin with small activities, and then we will gradually build up to more significant changes that you can experiment. Throw away any mistakes you may have had and start fresh the next day. Trying to connect with meaningful experiences gives you a jolt of inspiration. We are guided by how things make us feel. With your goals floating around in your mind, let them simmer a little bit while we create a living space.

This begins with one enormous clean-up. We use minimalism and create space to help purify your daily thoughts. We all have one room where we sit down and do some tasks. These tasks could include reading, browsing the internet, writing, doing business, etc. Change that space and it will do something that will click inside you, giving you pleasure and happiness. Throw out all that doesn't make you happy or makes you feel bad (feelings are head and centre again). There are a lot of distractions that keep us from diving into our goals.

Go through your calendar with a fine-tooth comb. You'll notice how frequently you are side-tracked and wasting your time. The approach I want you to take is as follows:

- Don't get offended by people's opinions anymore.
- Stop the game of comparison and live your own life.
- Be YOU at home and at work. Take the mask off.
- Stop thinking all the time and just follow your intuition.

It will be almost too easy that your mind can decide to opt-out and reframe a mindset. Often, the best recommendation is the simplest, and it's the little stuff you don't do that restrains you from having the transformation you've always wanted— and definitely need.

The following mindset change hacks are an extra bonus, which when accompanied with the 7 hacks mentioned at the end of the book are a powerful source. You will need to read the whole book - or if listening to the audio, listen to it in its entirety to gain the full value.

Bonus Hack - 30 day Mindset Change 1

Get an empty small glass jar – you want to be able to see what's inside and have it within easy reach. Every day you will write a short note, word, or sentence and place it in the jar. It needs to be a positive, progressive thought to encourage you to stay on track with your: diet, business plan, gym routine, office work, new career, exam revision or any or personal goals.

It could be any of the following;

Day 1   - Excited and looking forward to tomorrow.
Day 2   - Easy Peasy!
Day 23 - Still loving it!
Day 24 - Committed!
Day 25 - I love reading.

Every day you will add another small slip of paper with a positive note. At the end of each month, you will look back at all the notes and reflect how far you have come. The goal is more about the journey and less about the destination.

Bonus Hack - 30 Day Mindset Change 2

Find a calendar with enough space to write a short word or sentence under each day and place it on your wall. Every night before you get ready for bed, reflect on the day that has come to an end and write about it on the calendar.

Alternatively, create a morning routine and produce a form of gratitude and thanks for the day ahead. This motivates you to keep progressing along as well as encouraging you to continue taking action in your daily life.

As you visibly see the calendar on your wall, you will notice how your daily goals are manifesting tangible change into your life. Recording this is a way to recognise that change is happening, especially when it is often difficult to feel a difference.

Bonus Hack - 30 day Mindset Change 3

Choose 1 day each month where you do nothing but provide yourself a day of self-care. I suggest going to a local spa, or a gym with spa facilities such as: a swimming pool, Jacuzzi, steam room and sauna. Perhaps go for a haircut at your favourite salon or get a beard trim from the coolest barber in your city. Treat yourself to a pedicure, or a relaxing day in the park. Read a book and have a nice meal. This serves two benefits. First, you get to relax and enjoy a full day of small, self-indulgence; and second, you can reward yourself for staying on track with your goals and behaviour changes. This can help you associate hard work with a little bit of play.

Chapter 1: Positive Thinking/ Mindset – An Introduction

"Don't be pushed around by the fears in your mind. Be led by the dreams in your heart." - Roy T. Bennett

---

1.1 Introduction

Positive thinking is a mental attitude where positive results are expected. Increasingly, courses and books about this concept are attracting more people. More and more successful people say that they achieve what they want because of their optimistic lifestyle. A person with a positive attitude - both professionally and socially - will always be more successful than a person who doesn't have control of his or her thoughts.

1.2 How to Apply Positive Thinking

It is not easy to change everything that you've learned in life. Immediately implementing positive thinking isn't that easy, but over time, you will get results. Use meaningful words when you speak. Instead of telling yourself "I can't," persuade yourself that you will do all you can.

For example, tell yourself:
- "I will do all I can to have a good friendship."
- "I will do all I can to have a brilliant career."

- "I will do all I can to keep myself safe."

Delete all negative feelings: If you are in a bad mood, do not let negative thoughts and feelings prevail. Eradicate stress each day by focusing on good things in your life.

Use terms that are powerful and successful: Fill your thoughts with words that make you feel powerful, happy and guided in the right direction.

Practice positive statements: Positive self-talk is one of the most common practices of positive thinking. Repeat a meaningful expression or mantra, like "I deserve to be happy," or "I deserve to be cherished." The more it's repeated, the more your brain changes to make it feel true.

Redirect your feelings and thoughts: A common method of psychotherapists is to redirect your thoughts in situations where you feel bad. To create a happier mindset, think of a positive image that you can go back to whenever your thoughts need to be redirected.

Start thinking positively and then you'll succeed: Nothing compares to self-confidence, which often leads to success. Put aside your fears and trust that your goals will be accomplished when you start thinking positively.

Examine what goes wrong: Though we stress that it's important to stay positive, being in complete denial is not a positive approach. If something goes wrong, take some time to identify the problem, discover what led to the current situation, and create a plan to avoid future mistakes. Just do not dwell on the problem for too long.

Please pardon yourself: If you continuously fight about things that go wrong, nothing will change. Tell yourself that you are forgiven, and you can continue.

Give failure a chance: Even the worst experiences in our lives can give us new, positive opportunities. For example, after losing your job, you might be able to start your own business or go back in school!

Based on your imagination: It can be a great motivation to imagine what you want to do, the ideal personality you want to have, and how to make it come to fruition!

Positivity doesn't always mean smiling and looking happy, it's more about your general outlook on life and your desire to concentrate on all that's good in life.

In this section, we will examine the fundamentals of positive psychology, identify many of the benefits of a positive approach to life, and explore several techniques to cultivate a positive attitude.

It's a long piece, so sit back and relax. You probably have an idea of what a positive attitude is, but starting with a definition is always helpful:

> *"Positive thinking is a mental and emotional disposition, focused on the bright side of life and anticipating positive results," and "Positive thought means approaching the challenges of life in a positive way," says Kendra Cherry in Very Well Mind (2017). It does not necessarily mean preventing or avoiding ominous things, but instead leveraging potentially unfortunate circumstances to see the best in other people and looking at yourself and your talents positively."*

To have a positive attitude is to make good thoughts a habit, always find the silver lining, and to make the best of every situation.

1.3 The Traits of a Positive Mindset

We know what a positive attitude is, so it's time to immerse ourselves in the next important question: How is it achieved? A positive attitude is related to many traits and characteristics, including:

Optimism: A desire to try something rather than believing that your efforts aren't worthwhile.

Acceptance: To understand that things don't always work like you want them to, but to learn from your mistakes.

Resilience: A recovery from adversity, frustration and loss rather than abandonment.

Thankfulness: You continue to appreciate the good things in your life.

Consciousness: To dedicate the mind to conscious awareness and increase concentration.

Integrity: A truthful, respectable and straightforward trait rather than a disillusioned and self-serving one.

These traits are important to your positive way of life. Acting with hope, tolerance, courage, appreciation, compassion and honesty can enable you to develop and maintain a positive attitude.

A-List of Positive Attitudes: There are many more concrete examples of a positive attitude in practice if the above list is too vague. Positive attitudes can include:

- Loving the unexpected, even if you initially did not want it.
- Facing adversity in the eyes and still managing to laugh.
- Staying motivated with positive words and the people around you.

- Smiling – a simple way to reverse your mood and bring happiness to others.
- Getting back up after you fall. It doesn't matter how many times you fall, be your energy source that elevates you.
- Knowing the relation is more important than substance.
- Staying focused, even if it's hard.
- Remembering the good times, even if you lose. Be positive about the success of someone else.
- Having a positive vision for the future, regardless of how bad you feel now.
- Complimenting a stranger.
- Telling someone they did a great job and meaning it.
- Not whining- no matter how unfair things seem to be.
- Ignoring others' complaints and not allowing their disappointment to bring you down.
- Giving more than you expect in return.
- Being honest with yourself.

1.4 Positive Attitude is the Key to Success

We know that a positive attitude feels great, but how can you get one? What makes a positive attitude so significant, so impactful, and so life-transforming? The characteristics mentioned above provide us with an idea of the benefits.

Don't worry; this book isn't about the kind of positive thinking where nothing can ever go wrong. Optimism isn't warranted in every case, every minute of the day.

Right-thinking does not always mean joy or satisfaction, and it doesn't mean that you must disregard something negative or disagreeable in your life. It involves integrating both the positive and the negative into your perspective and choosing optimism in general.

When negative things arise, you won't always be satisfied and will need to learn to accept bad moods and harsh emotions. You can't control your mood, and you can't always control your thoughts, but you CAN choose how you handle the situation. You will eventually become miserable if you choose to give in to the world's negative, cynical, gloom-and-doom view, and you may also miss a significant opportunity to grow.

Accommodating Negative Thoughts and Negative emotions

According to psychologist Barbara Fredrickson, you should concentrate on risks, threats and vulnerabilities. This was important for the survival of our ancestors, after all.

Positive thoughts and feelings, on the other hand, "expand and create" our tools and abilities, and open up more possibilities for us (Fredrickson 2004).

You do not need to be annoyingly optimistic when building the foundation for your positive thoughts, but rather have trust in yourself and your future. It is all right to feel pessimistic, but in the long run, choosing to respond with hope, confidence and gratitude will help you much more.

Apart from developing your skills and personal resources, there are many other advantages to maintaining a positive attitude - including improving overall well-being and building stronger stress management capabilities. According to experts in the Mayo Clinic, positive thinking will enhance your life, minimize depression and stress levels, give you more immunity to the common cold, improve your overall psychological and physical well-being, boost your cardiovascular health and protect you from cardiovascular disease.

Benefits of Positive Mindset and Attitude at your Workplace

Nothing captures a positive attitude in the workplace more than Psychological Capital (PsyCap). This multi-component framework is composed of four psychological resources. Luthans and Youssef in

2004, renowned management and leadership researchers, created the positive and developmental states of an individual, the four characteristics being: Hope, Efficacy, Resilience & Optimism, known shorter as the PsyCap, is a "positive psychological asset." Their theory quickly spread amongst supportive therapists in the institutions, and by 2011, hundreds of PsyCap references were already written.

The Four 'PsyCap Positive 'components:

Hope – Where motivation & power to take action in goal planning intersect.
Efficacy – Ones own belief in confidence to achieve specific goals
Resilience – The ability to overcome adversity, stress, conflict, failure and change
Optimism – Not fixed to negative events, but optimism reinforces efficacy and hope

The first formal study of PsyCap was conducted in 2011, and it highlighted several of PsyCap's many advantages at work. PsyCap was positively related to job satisfaction, organisational engagement and emotional well-being.

PsyCap also had a good relationship with corporate citizenship (desirable employee conducts) and various performance measures (self-assessed, manager ratings and objective actions).

The positive attitudes of the company and workers, such as motivation and resilience, seem to bring positive results. For greater impact, we suggest the same positive-psychological states being utilised within an individual's life outside of the workplace!

A further study of the relationship between satisfaction and benefits for workers was done by giants of positive psychology (Sonja Lyubomirsky, Laura King and Ed Diener, 2005). They showed that positive attitudes in the workplace favour the employee because happy workers are more successful than other unhappy employees.

What is PsyCap?

Psychological Capital or PsyCap is defined as

"An individual's positive psychological state of development"
It's characterised by:
- Having the self-assurance needed to put in the required effort to succeed at challenging tasks;
- Feeling positive about succeeding not just in the present, but also in the future;
- Persevering towards accomplishing goals;
- Being flexible enough to redirect goals to succeed;
- Having the ability to bounce back when beleaguered with obstacles and adversity.

PsyCap focuses on the application of positive psychological concepts in the workplace through measurable traits.

In an organisational context, the PsyCap anchors its theory on four pillars: HOPE, EFFICACY, RESILIENCE, and OPTIMISM. These four pillars (with its fetching acronym, HERO), are closely linked to job satisfaction and life satisfaction.

Hope – Where motivation & power to take action in goal planning intersect.
Efficacy – Ones own belief in confidence to achieve specific goals
Resilience – The ability to overcome adversity, stress, conflict, failure, and change
Optimism – Not fixed to negative events, but optimism reinforces efficacy and hope

The Benefits of PsyCap in the Workplace

The idea of Psychological Capacity was specifically designed for organisations. Its pioneer, Fred Luthans, theorised that organisations best benefit from focusing less on educational development and zeroing-in more on psychological development.

Why so?

Luthans argues that human resources are as much a competitive advantage (as access to proprietary technology, brand image, or the ability to manufacture products at the lowest cost) because they are harder to mimic – much harder than financial or physical resources.

Employees or members of an organisation possess two types of knowledge:

EXPLICIT / OVERT
IMPLICIT / TACIT

Explicit or overt knowledge are abilities, skills, and competencies acquired from education and experience.

Implicit or tacit knowledge, on the other hand, is knowledge acquired over time through socialisation in an organisation.

It's the latter that offers a long-term competitive advantage in the workplace because it is unique to the organisation. It's amassed through time and cannot be transferred to or acquired by competitors.

This is why Luthans cautions companies to capitalise on human capital management by focusing on building implicit knowledge.

High levels of PsyCap are closely related to job satisfaction and employee performance. This is very evident most especially in the services industry. In addition, employees who strive at work can safely be assumed to feel more fulfilled, thanks to the relationship between job satisfaction and life satisfaction. Even physical health is positively affected. When a higher level of PsyCap is identified, individuals have also been found to have lower cholesterol and BMI levels.

How does PsyCap apply in Coaching and Leadership?

Does success make you happy? Or is it the other way around?
American author, speaker, and positive psychology advocate, Shawn Anchor (2011) believes it's the former. If an organisation possesses hope, resilience, and optimism, it is most likely to endure a challenging work environment.

Thus, when success is achieved in the workplace, the satisfaction and the ability to overcome adversity are huge contributing factors to happiness.

This is precisely the reason why PsyCap is becoming important in any coach or leader's training arsenal.

HOPE

Hope and positivity are personality traits closely linked to physiological and psychological well- being.

Hope is a cognitive process. It motivates a person to find the will and the ways and means that lead to positive emotions. And it certainly doesn't mean donning an unrealistic hope that everything will turn out fine.

Here's why…

Hope can be viewed as a process consisting of three components.

1. Goals
2. Pathways
3. Agency

Professor Snyder discovered that hopeful people are those who see many pathways to goals because they anticipate obstacles. Hopeful people, according to this theory, don't expect the journey to be easy.

How does one hope? How do you put hope into practice?
First, decide on the goal you want to work on. Your goal must be something you care about.
It must be specific and measurable.

It must also have a deadline.

Write it down. Contemplate on how it would feel to reach this goal.

Second, develop a pathway. How will you reach your goal? Often enough, your goal will consist of subgoals.

Develop a variety. Do you have a plan A? Plan B? C? D?

Hopeful people ANTICIPATE obstacles and know that the process won't always be easy-peasy. When people visualise obstacles, they make concrete plans. And when you make concrete plans, you are more likely to reach your goals.

Having alternative plans not only ensures success, it also allows you more energy. This is because you know that a setback is just a delay. It won't stop you from achieving your goals, nor would it demoralise you.

Also, discern if you are trying to overcome an obstacle. Most of the time, people merely need to "pummel through". In that case, you must factor in mental and physical exhaustion, as well.

Third, develop a high level of agency. Foster an environment that enables you to persist and sustain motivation. Find ways to keep energised. Get your happy and creative juices flowing so that you can come up with unique plans of action.

Remember, hope isn't just a sunny disposition. It isn't hoping that things will turn out for the best. Rather, it's a process of setting goals, evaluating pathways, anticipating obstacles, and overcoming them.

It's a growth process with plans. In fact, it allows for struggle and growth.

Hope is an IF-THEN route.

If _____

then I will _____

And in the event you find yourself losing passion, or if you've exhausted alternative pathways, hope also means looking at alternative goals. These alternative goals will then serve as your jump-off point to reaching your goal.

SELF-EFFICACY

Self-efficacy is defined as:

"People's beliefs about their capabilities to produce effects."
The confidence, the belief that we can take on the challenge… the belief that we have what it takes to overcome challenging tasks, influences how we think and feel. It has a great bearing on self-motivation.
When we believe that we already possess the ability to produce the desired outcome, we have a major incentive to act NOW! The higher we think of our abilities, the harder we work to reach our goals. This alone leads to a higher success probability.
How does one build efficacy?

1. Recall past successes

When you look back on past successes, you increase self-confidence. Coaches and leaders often lead students to increase awareness by appreciating success stories instead of creating them. Why so? This is because by focusing on success, you inevitably outline the strengths, traits, and factors that contribute to success.

2. Mimic other people

When you see others overcoming difficulties and challenges, you increase your belief that you can do the same. This works especially when you find parallelisms with yourself and your role model.

3. Foster an environment that would set you up for success

Words (verbal persuasion) can be a great source of confidence. But for you to also overcome self-doubt, you need to set an environment that ensures success. Structure situations that would set an organisation up for success. Take into consideration that the people you place must also be ready. It is common to see people fail - not because they couldn't do tasks - but because they were prematurely placed in situations where they were likely to fail.

4. Alter your perspective on failure and negative experiences

How you interpret your physical and emotional responses to stressful situations influences how you judge your susceptibility to stress. People with good levels of self-efficacy tend to see reactions as an "energising enabler". In brief, how you perceive obstacles greatly impacts how you deal with them. Resistance, fear, and fatigue are all normal responses. But rather than "lack of confidence" or weakness, you can also view such responses as excitement or curiosity. A change in view can significantly improve performance and eventually, efficacy.

RESILIENCE

Resilience is the ability to bounce back from adversity. It's also the ability to grow stronger from overcoming negative events.

Hardship and rejection are part of life. But what determines success isn't defined by how frequently we get rejected. Rather, it's how often we bounce back and get back on the groove.

In effect, resilience is about learning how to fall and rise.

How does one go about building resilience?
As per Senior Editor Diane Coutu (2002), resilience is made up of these practices:

1. Learning to Face Reality

It's difficult to think positively when faced with hopelessness and despair – which is why the best thing to do is face reality. Expecting things to get better soon (and realising soon enough that it won't) can zap energy and hope from anyone. Thus, in difficult instances, accepting failure, rejection, and difficulty for what they are may be a better step to take to endure for the meantime.

2. Searching for Meaning

Resilience is finding meaning and purpose when faced with a situation that cannot be altered. A lot of energy is spent fearing what cannot be controlled. Ask, what is this roadblock teaching me? What can I do better next time? Be of the mindset that this setback's lesson is preparatory for something even bigger and more significant.

3. Learning How to Improvise

Your ability to bounce back can be gleaned from the way with which you face a situation with whatever you have at the moment. It isn't so much the tools or the resources you have. It's the ability to create new ways to reach a goal. The best leaders are masters at this.

OPTIMISM

Optimism is all about acknowledging the likelihood of success now and in the future. Optimists believe that good things will happen to them – regardless of their situation.

To develop optimism, you must change your focus. This can be done by acknowledging and accepting the past, appreciating the present, and seeing the future as a place of opportunity. Why all this focus on the "past"? The answer lies in perspective. When you change your perception of the past, you affect how you see the impact it has on the future. Coaches use "reframing" as a technique in coaching and therapy sessions. The past cannot be changed, but it can be used as a stepping stone for future plans.

Furthermore, optimism is a smorgasbord of positive responses. You cannot control your initial reaction. But you certainly can control your RESPONSE.

For instance, angry frustration from rejection is a reaction.

But you can change your response by keeping in mind how even the most negative settings have a silver lining. (There could be a better opportunity waiting in line!)

Practice gratitude despite the negativity because everything is a learning experience. Toxic work culture? Surround yourself with positive people. Remember that even the good life has its downs. Psychological Capital is closely linked to wellbeing, work, satisfaction, and happiness. Developing just one in the HERO pillars (hope, efficacy, resilience, and optimism) already positively impacts employees / members.

1.5 Positive mindset and Leadership

Just as a positive attitude is vital to rank and file, it is easy to understand why leaders need a positive attitude as well. Experts Hannah, Woolfolk and Lord (2009) proposed a model for effective leadership based on the idea of "the right thing" being able to bring people together with a good sense of self-improvement. In this concept, a leader with a positive attitude is more likely to be better performing and more involved. Through role modelling and social influence, they are also better suited for leading others to have a more positive attitude.

Another set of research conducted at the same time confirmed the relationship between the leader and the followers; management trust affected PsyCap positively and had a major impact on leaders' and followers' success.

Management trust is also related to successful leadership and achievement. Although faith in management does not necessarily indicate that both leaders and supporters have a positive mindset, it benefits to have a positive workplace attitude.

Forbes author Victor Lipman (2017) puts observations like this in simpler terms: "You can always pursue someone with a positive mindset more easily." This means that a leader's positive attitude is going to attract followers and inspire encouragement and dedication in their subordinates.

Leaders have to be constantly "on" and spend a great deal of their time as a solid, confident leader. This job is tiring; it will enable leaders to remain positive and resilient in difficult situations.

Chapter 2: Ways to Achieve Positive Mindset

"A Positive mind always considers and so realise that even failure is a part of success." - Manna Sangma

---

In this chapter, we show you some of the most popular and proven methods to achieve a positive mindset. Larry Alton (Success.com) has shared some practical tips to help someone get motivated. Here are a few of his tips:

- Start the day with positive statements.

- Concentrate on good things; no matter how small they are.

- Even in bad situations, find humour.

- Transform shortcomings into lessons and learn from them!

- Convert negative self-speaking into some positive self-speaking.

- Concentrate on the present rather than dwelling in the past or losing yourself in the future.

- Ask friends, colleagues, family, contacts and networks to help and encourage you to find supportive peers, mentors and colleagues.

Brian Tracy, who is a successful author and speaker, adds a few more tips in this regard. According to him, you should:

- Remember that your response determines the outcome of a situation.

- Chase down negative thoughts, using positive affirmations or phrases.

- Include motivational and optimistic statements in your life.

- Be pleased, thankful and carry on the best of intentions for the people around.

- Challenge yourself if something goes wrong.

- Show the world how strong and optimistic you are!

One should also consider some of the tips from Megan Wycklendt, which she stated in Fulfillment Daily Newspaper. According to her:

- One should take their problems as a growth opportunity.

- It is great to be rejected. Rejection happens to everyone!

- To characterise life, one should use positive words.

- Replace what you will have with what you already have.

- Don't indulge yourself into the problems of others.

- Breathe! Intentionally, consciously and attentively.

- In times of tragedy and violence, remember that the right and good will happen.

- Utilise positive approach to overcome difficulties.

- Make others smile.

Moving forward, Dr Tchiki Davis's strategies can also motivate you to attain a positive attitude. You just have to ask yourself, "Do I really think positively?".

We have a checklist for you to do your own analysis so that you may examine where you are standing.

- Do you reinforce your positive thoughts by using positive words?

- Do you reinforce your brain's ability to deal with information using a positive approach?

- Do you enhance the ability of your brain to focus on the positive things in your daily routine?

- Do you practise appreciation?

- Do you try to savour every good moment?

2.1. Help Students Develop a Positive Mindset for a Positive Attitude

You can encourage students to try the above techniques and pass on the benefits of developing a positive mentality. However, there are some other ways students can become more efficient in improving their attitude towards education and school.

Elliot Seif, a well-known writer, discusses thirteen ways in which students can increase their concern about their education.

1. Build the element of hope among students. This allows students to understand the importance of working hard and provides them with more chances to focus on their areas of interest.

2. Include positive information regarding their strengths on their daily, weekly and annual reports. Criticize them less!

3. Make them think instead of relying on textbooks.

4. Focus on the strengths of students instead of their weaknesses. Help them see that "the glass is half-full" rather than "the glass is half-empty." Understand that not all students are strong in every area. Encourage them to explore their strengths and interests. Teach students that they should see failure as a learning opportunity. This will surely encourage them to refine and improve their work.

5. Encourage them to slow down the process of reading and focus on what they consider to be relevant.

6. Tell students to concentrate on lessons and subjects that help them develop skills.

7. Encourage students to ask and answer questions. They are fundamental to their learning environment and their school's culture.

8. Write clear explanations for key issues. In case directions weren't clear, let students know that no question is too little or too dumb to ask.

9. Provide students with several after-school programs. This will allow students to build and expand their interests.

10. Use survey teaching methods.

11. Consider taking learning interactions as far as possible.

12. Create more ways to integrate student interest in a subject. For example, you may wear all red (to represent communism) while delivering a lecture on a revolution.

13. Help students create paths for success. For this, you may take your students on field trips.

2.2. Games and Activities to Teach Positive Mindset Skills

If you are interested in some realistic ways of enhancing your positive attitude, you are in the right place! You can use various exercises to improve your positive thinking. Some of the best known are mentioned here!

- Music may place you in a positive state of mind, so take advantage of it.

- Express your gratitude and appreciation for everyone and everything good in your life. Write down your gratitude so that you remember. Literally, write them down!

- Get some air! It profoundly affects your mind - slowly but surely - and steers it back to an optimistic and peaceful place.

- Don't let people label you. You are far more than a label.

- Don't question your inner confidence.

- Engage in positive activities, such as meditation, yoga, biking, athletics or whatever you enjoy.

- Stay in control and try to change any bad thoughts that come to mind.

- Don't move too quickly or push yourself too hard; everybody struggles, and that doesn't mean you're not good enough.

- Pay attention to what you eat and make sure to choose a healthy and optimistic diet.

- Change yourself! Whether or not you want it, it's better to embrace positive change.

Moving forward, if you're more interested in some fun, play the following games so that you improve your thoughts.

The Glad Game

Have you ever lost a job or split up with a partner, only to dwell on negative thoughts about the incident?

In this game, first introduced by the Disney movie Pollyanna, the main character consciously cultivates positive thinking. The other players are encouraged to turn the feelings of the first person into constructive ones; for example, they can say something like, "Now that I've lost my job, I'm going to have more time for my side business." This game encourages you to find the silver lining amongst the dark clouds and look for possibilities instead of despair.

Egg Balancing Game

The balanced egg game can be challenging, but an essential lesson in constructive thinking and open-mindedness.

Set a raw egg onto a slightly textured tabletop for your players (use a tablecloth). Ask them to figure out a way to make the egg sit tall on the tabletop. You may think it's unlikely to happen, but you can guarantee that it will happen soon! Let them try for a while. It may work, but in the end, you will probably need to give them a little mound of salt to balance the egg. This is an important thing to remember - when you think outside the box, things that seem unlikely are often possible.

Hunt for Happiness

Have the players mention things that make their lives worth living or things that make them happy. Once everyone has a list ready, send them on a scavenger hunt to collect as many items as possible on the list. You can set your mark. You'll have to be creative to check off everything on the list, particularly abstract stuff like "love." In addition to your positive thinking, it will also motivate you to improve your creative thinking. More games and events are available to help kids develop a positive attitude. Give those activities a try if you are a teacher, mother, coach or anyone who communicates with children.

Positive Steps Towards Well-Being

You can interactively show what you have done or want to try by taking notes. You may boost your well-being by:

- Taking on a hobby or developing a new skill.
- Doing some work and helping other people relax.
- Maintaining a healthy balance between sleep and work.

2.3 Positive Thinking Methods

<u>For Kids</u>

It's a tough time to be a kid these days. Mental health issues previously within the exclusive domain of adults are now as much a concern for kids.

How does one prepare a child to face such negativity? How do you equip young children to better deal with peer pressure, frustration, as well as all sorts of negative emotions?

The quick answer lies in building up their confidence. A confident child is a child poised for success, good health, and happiness. They are most likely to bounce back from setbacks quickly and won't hesitate to seek the help of a trusted adult.

The key is YOU. Parents, guardians, and teachers play a pivotal role in building a young child's confidence and self-assurance.

Some effective strategies that you may want to incorporate are as follows:

1. Make sure they know that you love them unconditionally.

   How they perceive what you feel or think of them has an intense bearing on the way they see themselves. When you deal with a child or student, make sure they understand how you love and care for them despite the poor decisions they have made or even the mistakes they have done.

   Children can be brutal to themselves and one another. Avoid criticising them harshly and at no time should you shame them.

2. Seek their assistance by giving them "special" tasks.

   Age-appropriate tasks, in addition to classroom jobs and chores, help young children feel competent, useful, and responsible. The word "special" alone, is a confidence booster because it will make them feel that it isn't just a task for anyone.

3. Join them during play but let them take the lead.

   When you play with children, be in it. Engage and play just like you would as a child. Role-play with them. Roll around if you need to. Joining young children during play sends the message that they are important and worthy of your time and attention.

   Allow them to choose the activity. Let them initiate and lead. When children see that parents and adults enjoy their "me-led" activity, they will inevitably feel valued.

4. Ask them for their opinion and advice.

   Just as children-led play leads to making them feel valued, asking young children for their opinion on age-appropriate situations will accomplish the same. This shows that even adults need help… and that it's always ok to ask for help when they need it.

5. Praise them … appropriately!

Not all praise is good praise. Simply showering them with accolades won't be effective in the long-run and may even prove to be detrimental. When a young child deserves praise for a specific task that had been accomplished well, give them genuine, specific praise that focuses on their effort rather than results. For instance, give praise for diligently practising math, rather than getting an A. Avoid general praises such as "good job".

For Teens

To their credit, adolescence is a time of significant development both mentally and physically. Fresh connections are being made in the thinking and processing areas of the brain at the same time that other areas are "pruned" away. which is why most teenagers shoot from the hip without thinking.

The teen years come with demanding situations that often result in pessimism and wrong choices. For a developing brain (and a body undergoing hormonal changes), the weight of school work, peer pressure, and extracurricular activities can set them on a path to negativity.

Here's how to encourage a positive attitude with teens.

1. Curb your negativity.

Parents and adults carry the world on their shoulders. But when your teen is around, curbing your negativity is a must! Let it begin with you. Get into the habit of seeing what can go right instead of what can go wrong. Focus on the little positive things, instead of the negatives. Teens mirror what they see.

2. <u>Encourage your teen to find a hobby or engage in activities they enjoy.</u>

Developing a teen's interests leads to building self-esteem. Support his or her interests even if you prefer another. For instance, if you'd rather she play the flute but she prefers percussion, let it go. Show up to performances. And avoid devaluing his choices such as "I wish you'd join the swim team like your brother."

3. <u>Encourage them to get physical</u>.

Everyone, young and old, benefits from regular exercise. Kids nowadays tend to sit in front of a screen or spend too much time thumbing through their phones. A consistent form of exercise not only benefits the body but the mind as well.

4. <u>Focus on acceptance and compassion.</u>

While building self-esteem develops confidence and positive thinking, a delicate balance must be had between the former and unattainable perfection.

Encourage acceptance of flaws. Let them acknowledge that everyone struggles and that what they see on social media isn't all that it seems. Everyone makes mistakes. Everyone wants to be accepted and admired. Focus on compassion by avoiding comparison. Teens tend to sense imaginary audiences. ("Everyone thinks I'm lame!) Thus, they become exceedingly sensitive to how others perceive them.

For those who work in the academe, you may want to tweak your classroom by:

- Keeping grades private
- Avoiding groupings according to ability

- Acknowledging small successes
- Providing opportunities to redo homework

5. Encourage acts of kindness.

Have your teen do something special for themselves and another person each day. This helps them think positively as it gives them something to look forward to daily.

6. Encourage gratitude

A daily journal to record the positive things that happened to them that day is a great way to grow a positive mindset. We tend to look at situations differently when times are rough. But if we have reminders of how things have been going right for us, then perhaps, life isn't as bad as it seems after all.

7. Encourage a part-time job.

This is a practical way to help build self-confidence, understand the world, develop early stages of working life, and also begin the practice of money management.

For Parents

There are books, videos, talks, blogs, conferences, and seminars on parenting abound. But nothing ever prepares you for parenthood and all the worrying that comes with it.

It seems that parenthood and worry will always be in the same sentence. Parents worry about their children's health and welfare. Is he safe? How will this affect my marriage? My career? Am I giving my daughter enough time? Should I have forced myself to breastfeed? Should one of us stay home? Does this cough merit a trip to the doctor? My child is on the autism spectrum, will he be ok? How do I shield my child from bullying and substance abuse? The list is endless.

As a soon-to-be parent, new parent, or future parent, know that you aren't the only one grappling with these fears. Here are some of the more common fears and how to calm them.

1. *"I know I'll just end up hurting my baby!"* – Newborns are delicate, but they aren't teacups. The possibility of dropping your baby or giving him too much medicine is highly unlikely. Just as you'd prepare for an office presentation, knowledge is power, and practice makes perfect. If you're iffy or feeling uncertain about something, call your paediatrician. They've heard it all. Further, success favours the prepared. Seek parent friends and ask for advice. Read up and attend newborn orientation sessions at your local centre. Fears amongst new parents are fears of the unknown. But once you get your knowledge tank filled, you'll feel so much more confident knowing that you're doing things right.

2. *"A baby might rock my relationship with my husband/wife/partner"* – We've seen one too many happy relationships go sour after so many nights caring for a newborn. If you're worried sick about this happening, accept that a baby will change the dynamics in a relationship. You went from partners/husband-wife to mum and dad with a whole new set of responsibilities and expectations. But rather than seeing the baby as the constant third wheel, look at him/her as the next step in your relationship. Your love hasn't diminished. It has only changed in form. Sure, date nights will be replaced with nursing a sick child, or folding laundry. But this is the time when love and affection are needed the most. Moms will appreciate the extra hours of sleep. And in the meantime, dads can take up a few chores at night or during the weekends. Arrange for a few hours of "couple time" a few nights during the week. Appreciate one another for the hard work involved with having a baby.

3. *"I'm not used to this. I might go into depression and I fear I won't bond with my baby."* The magical feeling is real. But for many parents, maternal or paternal love won't kick in immediately. And that's OK! For women most especially, many changes occur during pregnancy. As if bodily changes weren't enough, they'd

have to grapple with a change in family dynamics and a change in career as well. Further, navigating the path to caring for a newborn isn't for the faint of heart. If you feel overwhelmed or if you think you or your partner is experiencing the baby blues or Post-Partum Depression (PPD), please know that you aren't alone. Changing hormone levels, a lack of sleep, and a whole new world of responsibilities can put anyone on the edge. Give your doctor a call. PPD is real and should be given proper medical attention.

<u>For Women</u>

Women are more likely to experience anxiety more than men. Whether we chalk it up to differences in brain chemistry and hormonal fluctuations, women face a life marked with hormonal changes linked to anxiety and major milestones that affect them more profoundly than men.

Biologically, men and women experience (and react) to events in their lives differently. But it may also be significant to note that social factors have a lot to do with women's anxieties. It begins early in life. Boys are encouraged to be independent and assertive, whereas girls are deterred from exhibiting such behaviour. Boys are encouraged to take on more risks at the playground, while girls are almost always told to stay away from danger. These little nuances result in girls feeling more vulnerable than boys. Because the message is this… girls can't cope on their own.

Later in life, the same message resonates in the workplace and at the homefront. They're expected to stay home (even if they earn more in the workplace) to care for the children. It's unspoken but they're expected to raise kids, do the housework while keeping a full-time job. And as if that weren't enough, gender inequality in the workplace is real. Men tend to be trusted more and paid more even if the women have the same skills in place.

It's an uphill battle for a lot of women. But their voices are now being heard. If you're a woman facing such anxieties, here are a few tips:

1. Throw "perfection" out the window - Women wear many hats: wife, mother, sister, friend, boss, employee, volunteer. There are only so many hours during the week, and perfection is an ideal best reserved for Instagram. Instead, set your priorities. Know your essentials and non-essentials then work from there. For instance, you don't need a picture-perfect kitchen. There are chores you could put off for the week (or even a month). Need help? Ask for it. You don't get a trophy for doing everything yourself. If you've kept mind, body, and soul together, you've done a good job.

2. Break tasks into chunks – If you're feeling overwhelmed, chances are you've been dreading a list of tasks you need to do before the day (or week) ends. Women are no strangers to that heart-thumping feeling of dread as they see upcoming deadlines and meetings. Even a visit to the gym or a date with the doctor seems like a threat! The result is decreased blood flow to the brain.

   Don't multitask. Break your tasks into chunks. If that isn't possible, view your task one step at a time. Remind yourself that achieving your goals is possible even when you can only take one small step at a time.

3. Its all about you and your own picture of you – Positive self-talk works wonders. Talk to yourself the way you would to a good friend. "If they can do it, so can you." If you involve mental imagery, so much the better! Martial artists improve their reaction times by 20% when they visualise themselves executing a good performance. The science behind this is focus. When you picture yourself doing exactly what you want to do (whether it be asserting yourself more in the workplace, working more efficiently, executing a gym exercise), you tend to follow through with the imagery.

For Men

Men won't admit it, but a lot of them suffer from anxieties too. It's different for everyone but the most common risk factors for men developing anxiety or depression include:

- A significant change in civil status or living arrangements (separation, divorce, death of a spouse)
- Physical health issues
- Relationship problems
- Loss of work
- Issues at the place of work
- Pregnancy and birth of a baby
- Drug and alcohol use
- Bullying

Among all these issues, work and the workplace seem to have the most significant impact on the mental health of males. Factors that contribute to job-related anxieties include high demands, work pressure, overload, an unclear work role, job insecurity, long working hours, bullying, and low job control. Physical signs of anxiety may include restlessness, panic attacks, insomnia, shortness of breath, a racing heart, muscle tension, and even vertigo.

The most important thing for men to know is anxiety and depression are not weaknesses.

An action plan for anxiety can cover a wide range of choices. Include exercise and stress management. Make sleep an "appointment" and not something to forego. Talk to a medical practitioner. These are real mental issues and not something you "get" because you aren't strong enough.

Try to include activities and hobbies that you enjoy. Look after your body by eating healthy, staying active, and getting plenty of sleep.

Avoid drugs and alcohol – even if it helps you block the negative feelings in the meantime.

If you are supporting someone with anxiety, here are ways for you to help them:

- Listen without judgment. Let them know that you're there to listen without being judgmental.
- Offer to go with them to doctor's appointments.
- Encourage them to get enough sleep and exercise.
- Don't pressure them into participating in activities. Instead, encourage them to go out and spend time with family and friends.
- Have a doctor and hospital number ready just in case you notice that they become a threat to others or themselves. Numbers that you should have handy include a GP's, a psychologist, a psychiatrist, and a suicide hotline.

Avoid giving them more anxiety by telling them to "snap out of it". (If they could, they would've done so a long time ago). It's mighty unhelpful to stay away or avoid them for fear of "hurting" them. Avoid telling them they just need to stay busy or that they need to wipe away what they feel by going to a party.

Another issue that may cause anxiety in men is age. Older men are no strangers to anxiety for different reasons. It could be because of an increase in health issues (prostate cancer, stroke, dementia, heart disease), chronic pain, losses (loss of work, loss of income, loss of mobility), social isolation, and a significant change in living arrangements (moving from an independent living arrangement to an assisted care facility).

With all these issues, it helps to get in touch with a medical professional and support group. What you're feeling isn't unique to you. Learn more from your doctor. You don't have to put up with this for the rest of your days. Help is available.

For Adults / Professionals

Do you feel like a slave to the clock? Is the anxiety you feel from work affecting your quality of life? Is the angst affecting your dynamics at home?

Work and daily life can throw even the most resilient adult/professional off balance. At home, triggers can include a never-ending list of chores to do, children or ageing parents who may need special attention, lack of support from a spouse or even finances. At work, triggers may include short deadlines, difficult superiors, and difficult coworkers. On the social front, it could be making small talk, public speaking, having to talk to authority or "important" people… And for most of us, there is that eternal expectation to outperform, overachieve, save, and invest.

Just where do you fit in being calm and composed in all this, when the pressure to perform seems to be breathing down your neck?

Here are a few strategies to get you managing anxiety whatever your circumstance:

1. Breathe! – That all too familiar feeling when your hands sweat or that thump-thump in your chest as you confront an event is your body's response to stress.

What to do? Practise focused deep breathing. Breathe in for a count of 4. Breathe out for another count of 4. Practice for a total of 5 minutes. By levelling or evening out your breath, your heart rate slows, calming you down.

2. Develop a meditation practice - Meditation is an ancient tradition practised to create a sense of calm and inner harmony. It has ties to many religious teachings, but meditation is more about finding awareness and peace rather than faith.

There isn't a right or wrong way of meditating. You may be familiar with its types:

- Mindfulness meditation
- Mantra meditation
- Transcendental meditation
- Focused meditation
- Movement Meditation
- Mantra meditation

Find a style that suits you. For starters, the easiest to begin is mindfulness meditation, the most popular meditation technique in the West. This involves simply paying attention to your thoughts as they pass through your mind. You simply observe for that particular time. Running an errand? You can meditate by being aware of every moment. Make each gesture count. Even a simple task such as washing the dishes can be a form of meditation as you go through the motions. Mindfulness meditation is a quick favourite because you don't need a guide to teach you and this type can easily be practised alone.

3. <u>Keep things in perspective</u> –The feelings of being overwhelmed and overloaded, combined with feeling misunderstood and under-appreciated, can set you on a downward spiral. The best way to manage anxiety is to keep things in perspective by focusing on the facts.

Is an objective causing you too much anxiety? Perhaps it's unattainable only because the tasks that lay ahead seem overwhelming at this time. If so, break them into chunks. Are your objectives reasonable and time-bound? Is it feasible considering the time and resources that you have at the moment? If not, consider breaking your goals into chunks and steps.

4. <u>Take care of yourself</u> - Get enough sleep. Sneak in a few days of physical exercise each week. Load your plate with the right types

of food. You're better equipped dealing with the stress-filled work environment if your body is up to it as well.

Imagine having to pull in a late night with an aching back. Or running on fumes just when you have to field questions from superiors. Get therapy if you need it. View sleep as you would an important meeting. And rest when you need to.

5. <u>Avoid multitasking</u> – Technology is supposed to make daily life easier. But the contrary seems to have happened. We think we can do several tasks all at once because of apps and time-saving devices, but that is farthest from the truth. When we do several things all at the same time, we only add fuel to the fire. We become more overwhelmed. And since our brains aren't wired to doing several things at once all the time (such as driving along the freeway whilst engaging a client for a potential sale), we end up doing one task less satisfactorily… sometimes to the detriment of life and health! If you're behind the wheel, focus on the road. If you're at work or school, list down the things you need to do that day. When you focus on a single activity, the focus itself distracts your mind from the anxiety.

6. <u>Don't be an all-or-nothing Annie</u> – Have you ever found yourself beginning a task (say clearing out the garage), only to give up soon as you start because it seems like an overwhelming undertaking? You're not alone. Rather than do everything on a one-time, big-time basis, chop your objective into chunks. Do a drawer here. Declutter a box over there. Need to gain/lose weight? Don't focus on the 15 stone you need to lose. Break your goal into a stone or even half a stone. When you accomplish small goals, completion gives you the confidence to repeat the process. Small goals count. And progress is progress no matter how small.

7. <u>Practice an attitude of gratitude</u> – There is always something to be thankful for. Some people would rather see the glass as half full. Go a step further and be thankful that you even have a glass! Make it a habit to express appreciation for the big and small things alike. Maintain a journal and jot down the things you are thankful

for daily… hot running water, waking up, warm coffee, your baby's giggle, that pleasant walk through the office garden. Find that person who makes a difference in your life and send a thank you note. Not a letter-writing person? Do something for someone whom you know can't pay you back. Buy breakfast for someone on the street. Volunteer for a soup kitchen. Teach someone to read. Finding the good in the daily grind will help you view the world differently.

Chapter 3: Positive Thinking Techniques to Gain Achievements

"We become what we think about."
-Earl Nightingale

Promote positivity at the beginning of the day. Sometimes, in the morning, you notice an unfavourable feeling. This unwanted feeling can instil bad thoughts in your mind. You can bear these feelings all day, which will make you pessimistic. Positive thoughts in such situations are the key to success. You must note that negative thinking is not helpful — moreover, a motivated "you" will result in a more productive day.

Concentrate on good things, but also face your difficulties, and you will find life flows much more smoothly. You might have difficulties focusing on academic tasks some days. You may come across some social issues. You must focus on methods that seem to work in these situations. If it is difficult to write a part of a project, for instance, then focus on a different area. No matter how hard the situation is, you must trust in the power of the good.

Humour is the best drug for stress management. So, if you have trouble with stress, watch comedy movies for laughter. In addition to refreshing your mind, this will help make a change to stagnant days.

Learn from your mistakes. There is no successful individual who hasn't failed. The good and successful people learnt from mistakes and never gave up. People who become demoralized from errors cannot succeed. Therefore, it is important to learn from your failures.

When you complete a job, you must assess how you did. The points that seem to hinder your advancement must be established. It will help you plan the next time you sit down and try the mission. You will achieve good results if you believe in positive power.

You must have a vision, commitment and power of positivity to achieve success. In addition, it can motivate you to achieve your objectives. You must, therefore, try to visualize what you want in life. You have to imagine the difficulties and ease into the quest for success.

In your personal or professional life, you may have some regrets. In turn, your future performance can be greatly affected. Ideally, you will learn to forgive yourself here. In such a situation, you have to tackle the negative thinking and try to overcome it. You have to accept your errors and remind yourself that everybody makes mistakes. It is necessary for you to succeed in overcoming regrets.

You may have concerns regarding past or future issues. Stay focused on the present. The consequence is that you are still sorting mistakes from the past and worrying about the future. The best time to live in is the present. Concentrating on the moment will help you take the right steps. The right steps are important for success, and ultimately that is what you want.

Stay in positive social circles. Socialise with positive friends and people. This gives you positive feelings that are vital to your success. You must, therefore, try to make friends who have positive power. In addition, you need mentors who will help you learn from your mistakes.

Impacts of Positive and Negative Brain Thinking

Positive behaviour affects the brain and will expand your mind. You have multiple positive emotions, including happiness, affection and satisfaction. It is obvious that you feel better with these feelings. Positive thinking allows you to see the world differently. This gives you more opportunities and allows you to discover the key to success.

How Does the Brain Suffer from Negativity?

You can do nothing except feel fear or rage in the face of a tense situation. This occurs when the mind is enveloped by negativity. It limits you to only one thing on your mind, which means you fail to figure out how the issue can be resolved. Your focus remains on life's worries (possible future outcomes). So, negativity impacts your positivity capacity and doesn't take you anywhere. In other words, it blurs your vision and prevents you from seeing things much more clearly.

Fixed Vs Growth Mindset

The most powerful thing you possess is your mind!

Your mind is a mighty weapon that could work for you or against you. What you tell yourself and believe about yourself can prevent change or allow for new skills and opportunities to flourish!

A link exists between and among your beliefs, habits, and achievements.

But let's cut to the chase... that link is all about your mindset.

What is a mindset?

A mindset is the sum of thoughts and beliefs that defines how you understand yourself, your immediate environment, and the world.

American psychologist and Lewis & Virginia Eaton Professor of Psychology at Stanford University, Carol S. Dweck theorised that there are two types of mindsets:

A Fixed Mindset
V
A Growth Mindset.

People with a Fixed Mindset believe that their qualities are static, fixed, and cannot be changed. These individuals suppose that their talents, temperament, level of creativity and intelligence are set. They feel that there is no use working to develop and learn. Further, they tend to believe that talent, more than effort, leads to success.

On the other hand, people with a Growth Mindset believe that talent, intelligence, creativity, and learning can grow given experience, effort and time. They believe that they can become smarter with effort. They also believe that effort influences success, so they put in extra time, and thus achieve more.

FIXED MINDSET

Pros	Cons
Prevents short-term failure	Impedes your ability to develop new skills, learn, and grow
People who practice a Fixed Mindset as regards to their sexual orientation -- meaning they accept who they are and who they're meant to be, are better adjusted than those who feel that they should "change".	Low tolerance for failure and temporary setbacks.
	Easy successes and wrong praise discourages a "can-do" mentality Cultivates an "I should look smart" attitude

GROWTH MINDSET

Pros	Cons
Helps build confidence because you are constantly learning something new	If used incorrectly, can lead the person to believe that effort is all you need. May encourage ineffective strategies.
Encourages growth and risk-taking	
Improves self-esteem, insight, and relationships	
Lessens stress, helps you bounce back quickly from setbacks, increases resilience	
Lowers risk of depression	
Allows you to see setbacks as learning experiences/opportunities for growth instead of permanent failure	
Allows you to enjoy the hard work because you know it leads to rewards down the line	

What We Have Learned from Children

Before the concept of Fixed and Growth Mindset became a global phenomenon for learning and development in the workplace, it was a study intended to discover students' attitude about failure. What makes some students rebound? Why are others devastated by even the smallest setbacks?

According to Professor Dweck, students who have a Fixed Mindset believe that their basic abilities, talents, and intelligence are fixed traits. They think that that's all they were born with and therefore, all they have.

Not surprisingly, they have a fear of looking daft because they don't believe that they can redeem themselves once others are impressed upon by their "unintelligence".

On the flip side, students with a growth mindset believe that abilities and intelligence can be cultivated with education, persistence, and effort. Their basic abilities are but a starting point. And while no two people are the same, they hold onto the idea that anyone can be smarter, better, and achieve more.

The difference between these two mindsets is as clear as night and day, but it isn't always easy to spot. Perseverance and a good work ethic are certainly prerequisites to success. How can anyone tell if this is only up to a certain point?

Professor Dweck explains this at a talk she gave to Stanford students in 2014. She introduced the "Power of Yet." In her talk, she mentions a high school in Chicago where students had to pass 84 units to graduate. But unlike many high schools in the same area, failing students were not given a failing grade. Instead, they got a "NOT YET".

It's a novel way of assessing a student. Getting a failing mark can easily make anyone feel lost and broken. But the "NOT YET" mark made those who didn't make the cut feel they were on a learning curve. "Isn't that wonderful?" Dweck said. With "not yet" you gave students a path to follow. NOT YET means you haven't failed. It simply means that you are on a path of learning and that you just haven't learned it yet.

<u>The Benefits of the Growth Mindset do not end within the walls of the schoolroom.</u>

The same theory applies to anyone at any age who wishes to learn and progress. Have you been wanting to learn to play an instrument? Do it, because you absolutely can! How about that course you've wanted to take? Just begin. It's never too late!

Malcolm Knowles developed the study of Andragogy in 1968. He described it as the art and science of helping adults learn. The four principles of Andragogy are as follows: 1st, that adults learn better from experience. 2nd, that adults favour a practical approach (problem-solving method) to apply what they learned to solve a particular problem. 3rd, that adults are interested in learning relevant concepts. And 4th, that adults need to be involved in the planning, as well as the evaluation of how they are taught.

All these show that adults amplify learning when they possess a Growth Mindset – finding the topic's relevance and seeking a solution to a particular problem.

Sharran Merriam, a professor of adult education at the University of Georgia, Athens, specializes in the Adult Learning Theory. In her paper, *Andragogy and Self-Directed Learning: Pillars of Adult Learning Theory,* she describes the adult learner as someone who:

1. Can direct his/her learning.
2. Has a tank of life experiences to draw learning from.
3. Has learning needs related to a changing social role.
4. Is problem-centred and interested in the immediate application of the knowledge learned.
5. Is motivated to learn by internal factors, rather than external reasons.

Her research reveals that for adults to acquire new skills, the above criteria must be met and that for learning to be maximised, the thrust must be problem-focused. The adult learner must also be motivated to learn not because he is required, not because he needs to impress others, but because he genuinely wants to learn and progress. Very Growth Mindset-esque!

How long does it take for adults to learn?

Speaker and author of *The Personal MBA*, Josh Kaufman doesn't believe it takes "10,000 hours to learn anything".

10,000 hours is what it takes to be an expert in a very competitive field. But to simply go from zero to "pretty good" takes as little as 20 hours. That's just the equivalent of 45 minutes every day for a month.

What does it take for an adult to learn? It isn't as complicated as we think.

- Practice the skill AT LEAST 20 hours.
- Remove barriers and distractions (as would anyone).
- Deconstruct what you need to learn.
- Keep an eye on what you are learning and absorbing. Learn sufficiently to correct yourself.

Growth Mindsets

Don't allow your beliefs to hold you back. If you find yourself naturally creeping towards a static frame of mind, keep these mantras where you can see them.

Growth Mindsets that could help you achieve your goals, not just by working harder, but working smarter:

1. *I can learn this / get better at this for as long as I keep trying*

People with a Growth Mindset don't quit at the first sign of difficulty or weakness. Rather, they believe that the more effort they put in, the better they become.

Here are 7 examples of iconic figures skyrocketed themselves to success with a growth mindset:

1. The first rejection hurts like no other. A second one is a punch in the gut. So, imagine how it must feel to have been rejected over a thousand times! This is exactly what happened to Harland David Sanders… better known as Colonel Sanders of Kentucky Fried Chicken. At 65, Sanders found himself bankrupt and down on his luck. What he had, however, was an excellent chicken recipe. And so, he drove around in his car convincing restaurant and diner owners to try his fried chicken recipe. In exchange, he asked a nickel as commission. He was turned down 1,009 times (yes, he counted it) before a lucky restaurant gave him a nod. Today, Colonel Sanders' KFC remains to be a legendary icon when it comes to fried chicken.

2. Elvis was phenomenal. But not too many people know that he endured failure after failure after failure. He failed his music classes. He was a social misfit as a young lad. To make ends meet, he worked as a truck driver while trying his luck with a recording career. One time, right after a paid gig, his manager told him that he wasn't going anywhere and that he was better off driving a truck. But Elvis persevered. His first few recordings ended nowhere, and he was also told that he couldn't sing. Eventually, his music caught on, and his records continue to sell years after his death.

3. It's inconceivable to think that Michael Jordan once thought himself a failure. But that's exactly what makes him successful. *"I have missed more than 9,000 shots in my career. I have lost*

almost 300 games. On 26 occasions. I have been entrusted to take the game-winning shot and I missed. I have failed over and over and over again in my life. And that is why I succeed."

4. Think about Stephen King, and you think about millions of books sold and movies that earned millions more worldwide. But King wasn't always a successful writer. Before he became a bestselling author, he had amassed a huge backlog of rejected stories. He had written his first novel, *Carrie*, while working as a teacher in rural Maine. He had enjoyed small successes selling short stories… but nothing anyone would consider building a career around just yet. He submitted *Carrie* 30 times. He was rejected 30 times. He had thrown in the towel when his wife asked him to try one more time. The rest is history.

5. JK Rowling is a great example of how success is possible if you just don't quit. Before *Harry Potter*, she had been battling depression. Her mother died unexpectedly and her first marriage was a failure. Alone and providing for herself and her young child, she was on welfare. She went to school and tried to work on a novel during her spare time. At a commencement speech, Rowling said

"Failure meant a stripping away of the inessential" At the end she added, "And so rock bottom became a solid foundation on which I rebuilt my life."

6. Walt Disney is a household name indeed. Children all over the world grew up with Mickey Mouse, wanting to visit the happiest place on earth. But this wasn't such an obvious prospect for the young Disney. When he was 22, he found himself fired from a job at a newspaper company in Missouri. His newspaper editor thought he lacked creativity. This didn't stop him from what he did best – creating illustrations. He later established a studio with his brother Roy, ventured into full-colour, Technicolor cartoons,

and later, amusement parks. Disney is now a brand name recognized around the world. Had he given up right then, the world wouldn't have Mickey and Minnie Mouse, as well as all those iconic characters generations of parents and children love.

7. Hellen Keller is an American author, lecturer, and political activist. She was the first deaf-blind person to earn a Bachelor of Arts degree. During her time, her accomplishments were unheard of even for someone without a disability. At 19 months, an illness (which is suspected to be meningitis or scarlet fever) left her both blind and deaf. But she learned to communicate with the help of Anne Sullivan, who was visually impaired herself. And because of her and Sullivan's persistence and perseverance, Helen went on to accomplish exceptional feats. For Helen, *defeat is simply a signal to press onward.* She did not let failure and closed doors deter her from publishing 12 books, and actively campaigning for the plight of the blind.

2. *I can't do it now. But it only means that I can't do it just YET.*

With consistent effort and mindful practice, anything can be learned. It's a great mindset for children as well as adults because one tends to take risks when you know that you can achieve an objective with hard work. With an attitude like this, you know that failure isn't the end… it simply means you haven't gotten there YET. You are on a path to learning. Every failure is simply a learning experience. It doesn't mean you CAN'T.

3. *It's never ever too late to learn*

Those who believe that you can't teach an old dog new tricks are in for a surprise. Sound scientific argument exists proving that the adult brain CAN absorb as much information as an impressionable child's brain. This is because the brain never loses the ability to learn and master new skills. The effort required to master a new discipline may just be more.

Recent studies by Dr. Dayana R. Touron, a professor of psychology, also show that older adults tend to practice "memory avoidance." This suggests that their ability to learn is largely affected by WILL rather than ABILITY. So, if you're an adult learner, by all means... take that course. Learn that instrument. Attend that class. All you need to do is want it and put in the needed hours to learn the skill. If you're still in doubt, just think about John Basinger. He managed to memorize the 60,000-word poem, *Paradise Lost*, at the age of 67 --- only because he wanted to complement his physical exercise with mental callisthenics. It took him nine years of practice (and you certainly don't need to achieve the same feat), but if his mind was capable of such achievement, then so can yours.

4. My failures are learning experiences. Even flops teach me something.

I have not failed. I've just found 10,000 ways that won't work. –
Thomas Edison

Nobody likes failure. But if you're reaching for an objective, a person with a Growth Mindset views failure as a great way to learn. Try again. If you should fail, fail better.

5. I look up to others who have been successful in their endeavours.

People with a Growth Mindset model their work after those who have been successful in similar work. Those with a Fixed Mindset, on the other hand, see these people as a threat and someone to envy.

This shouldn't be the case. Role models are the proof you need to show that it is possible. Instead of feeding an envy mindset, take an interest in their work and the manner with which they were able to achieve their own goals. You'd be surprised to find that they probably failed more times than you can imagine.

6. I value constructive criticism

People don't take negative feedback kindly. Helpful criticism can feel like an insult, putting people on the defence. So, how can you use negative feedback to your advantage?

Show gratitude – Acknowledge that you are receiving points of improvement

Analyse the feedback given - Take a look at your work and be objective. You may find the feedback to be helpful.

Ask questions – Sometimes, it just boils down to understanding what you were told. Ask for specific points of improvement.

Create goals – With a specific point of improvement in mind, set goals to include the feedback given.

7. The results of my attempts don't define me.

It's easy to be defined by low tests scores, a rejected proposal, and numbers that describe a particular status (weight, salary grade, etc). However, if you focus on these alone, you're allowing yourself to fall under a Fixed Mindset.

You are not your numbers. Focus on daily, consistent, positive habits. These inevitably lead to growth and development.

8. Being uncomfortable is OK.

A ship in harbour is safe. But that's not what ships are built for" goes a well-loved adage.

New challenges (or anything new for that matter) can be overwhelming only because of the unknowns and the probability of failure. This Fixed Mindset can lead anyone to simply avoid challenges.

But nobody accomplished anything worthwhile whilst staying within a comfort zone. When you accept the reality of humps, bumps, and detours, you are more likely to take a risk and pursue a path – despite the barriers.

9. If this doesn't work for me, I will try a different approach.

A Growth Mindset is not just about working harder but working smarter. There are different styles of learning. Find out which one is yours and stick to it. Some learn faster via a visual (spatial) approach. Some learn by an aural (auditory-musical) approach. And yet others maximise learning through logical (mathematical), physical (kinaesthetic), or verbal (linguistic) means. For instance, if a new skill involves historical memory work, perhaps it would help to visit the place instead of just highlighting words on a textbook.

10. I believe in myself and my capabilities!

When you feel confident with your ability to learn and grow despite the obstacles you face, you are more likely to persevere. Confidence helps you bounce back quickly after a setback….and that alone is very empowering!

Talk Yourself into a Growth Mindset

A Fixed Mindset can be devious. When you get frustrated and make a mistake, what do you find yourself saying? How about when faced with an overwhelming challenge, what's your knee-jerk reaction statement?

Here are some Fixed Mindset thoughts and Mind Growth samples of what to say instead.

Instead of ... (Fixed Mindset)
This is such a difficult math problem. I don't have the skillset for this.

Think ...(Growth Mindset)
I can learn this. I just might need a mentor's help / to acquire the necessary skills.

Instead of:
I'm not good at this.

Think:
Am I missing something? If so, what am I missing?

Instead of:
My plan didn't go as intended.

Think:
What are my alternatives? What's plan B? C? D? Good thing the alphabet has so many letters left! Who can help me? Where can I get the help I need?

Instead of:
I give up!

Think:
What do I want? Maybe I should just try a different strategy? Maybe I should try rewording this project's objectives. I'll give it another go.

Instead of:
My head's a mess and I can't calm my thoughts!

Think:
I'm teaching my mind to focus.

Instead of:
Hey! I got this! I'm the best!

Think:
I'm on the right track!

Instead of:
This doesn't make sense / It doesn't make sense to do this?

Think:
What will make it "have" some sense? It doesn't make sense ... YET.

Morning routines

Whether you find yourself wearing the hat of a student, office worker, supervisor, parent, business owner, teacher, or whatever role you play daily, there will be days when you feel you want to start over.

"If only life had a reset button," you wonder. "Or even a Ctrl-Z command. Now, wouldn't that be awesome?"

Guess what... life hands you exactly that every day when you wake up.

Whatever a morning is to you (whether you get up when the sun rises or just when the moon does), here are some morning routines you may want to use to get you started on the right mindset!

1. Prepare the night before. Mornings are a frenzy. Lessen the stress by laying your clothing out, prepping your gym bag, and prepping yours (and the kids') lunches. Clear your mornings of errands that can agitate and stress. I found the best for me was a to-do list written the night before. American Express CEO Kenneth Chenault writes down three things he wants to accomplish the following day.

2. Get enough sleep. In his TEDx Talk, Williams College Biology Professor Dr. Matthew Carter emphasized how sleep can make or break our lives. Incorrect sleeping habits or sleep deprivation can wreak the same havoc as smoking and eating

the worst types of food. Dr. Carter says that we should take our cue from our kids. Kids are the best sleepers because we give them a routine. We take the time to go to bed, bathe them, properly brush their teeth, read them a story, give them some water, turn of the lights… and they sleep very soundly once they do. Get a good night's sleep - it's key to waking up great the next day! Five to eight hours of sleep is ideal.

3. When you get up, make your bed immediately. William H. McRaven, a retired United States Navy admiral, has been known for these famous words, *"If you want to change the world, start by making your bed."* The act of fixing your bed sets the tone for the day because you've accomplished your first important task. It may seem like an insignificant chore, but it isn't! Making your bed reinforces the idea that the little things matter in life. If you come home to a bed that is made, you set the tone for the next day – even if today didn't go as planned.

4. Avoid social media. It's easy to lose track of time with all the notifications. Psychologist Wilcox Stephen is of the belief that social media sites such as Facebook can only increase self-esteem in the very short term. But it can incite us to keep up with appearances and mask our true personas. It can also feed anxiety as we subconsciously seek acceptance and approval via these media.

5. Use the few minutes of quiet to be thankful. Today is a new leaf – no matter how dreadful the day before was. An attitude of gratitude goes a long way, and there is always something to be thankful for!

6. Is a cup of coffee your go-to in the morning? Why not try lukewarm water instead? People with a positive outlook tend to reach for water (sometimes with a splash of lemon) instead of coffee because the results are astounding. It helps them feel more alert (versus coffee) as it rehydrates your body and jump-starts their metabolism. Studies suggest we can dehydrate

whilst asleep, and so water first thing in the morning is the best way to keep focused throughout the day.

7. Get your heart pumping at least three times a week. The wealthy and successful all prioritise health. Lift weights or head for the gym before anything else. Invest in an elliptical or treadmill. Prioritise and make time for physical exercise as you would an important appointment.

8. Meditate and set your intention – be in the moment. An excellent type of meditation anyone can do is simply being aware of what's happening in and around you. If you've got 5 minutes, you can meditate. Simply calm your mind. Don't think of tasks you need to accomplish just yet. Can't control your thoughts? Count your breath to focus. Haven't got 5 minutes? Be in the moment while going through your morning routine. Be conscious of the sound water makes or the whistling of the kettle. This is an excellent technique to calm down. Tranquillity helps elicit positivity.

9. Check your plate. A balanced breakfast gives your body just the right fuel to tackle your day. Always include protein, healthy fat, and fibre. A quick breakfast would consist of scrambled eggs on whole-grain toast with slices of avocado. Throw in some yoghurt with nuts or berries. A good breakfast not only boosts energy, it helps your concentration and memory as well. When your mind is at its peak, productivity is off the roof.

10. Read. Whether it's on the commute to work or just after a lovely shower and cup of strong coffee, sit down and spend 20 minutes reading every morning. Before you know it, you're reading a book a month. That's half the amount read per year by Barack Obama!

11. Practice chunking. Neuroscientist Daniel Bor explains that chunking is our ability to access or "hack" the limits of our memory. It's a method that allows people to take small pieces

of information and then combine them into meaning, easier-to-remember units. It's a great memory enhancer that you could do for a few minutes in the morning. Say, for instance, you want to remember items from a list. Form small groups that are similar (for instance, if trying to recall items from a grocery list, divide into dairy items, fresh produce etc). Chunking is an everyday memory enhancer.

12. Make time for happiness. Spend time with friends and family. This need not be a huge gathering ... even the simple act of eating breakfast together or making a quick call to a loved one can help boost your day.

Last but not least... smile. Smiling isn't just good for you; it positively affects others as well! A study by The British Dental Health Association showed that smiling can affect our mood dramatically. Feeling down? Forcing a smile can significantly improve your mood. It helps reduce the symptoms of anxiety such as digestion problems and elevated blood pressure. Also, smiling activates the neurotransmitters associated with pleasure – dopamine, serotonin, and endorphins. Your smile is a natural pain reliever and instant mood lifter! So, make the conscious decision every morning to be happy, grateful and respectful to others. Often those that don't smile need it the most.

The benefits of smiling don't end there. In a study conducted by the Face Research Laboratory (the University of Aberdeen in Scotland), men and women were more enticed by photos or images depicting people who smiled and made eye contact. They theorise that smiling makes you look more confident, sincere, attractive, and relaxed. And of course, when someone smiles at you, your immediate reaction is to smile back. Win-win.

Mindsets of Successful people – 7 Hacks:

When we see successful people thriving in their lives and endeavours (be it a business, sport, or project), we often wonder what is it that makes them achieve more. Successful people have many positive traits and habits. A common denominator for them is a positive outlook and a Growth Mindset.

Here's a peek into how they think ...

1. They know and accept themselves

Bill Gates and J.K. Rowling are introverts. But that didn't stop them from excelling in their fields. They know their strengths and accept their weaknesses. If they don't possess a skill set necessary to accomplish a goal, they either find someone who does or create ways and means to achieve it.

2. They set goals that are in line with their values, interests, skills, strengths, and purpose

Steve Jobs, Martin Luther King Jr, Nelson Mandela all lived their lives based on what they valued and what they were good at. Some had to pay a high price for pursuing their goals, but we doubt that any of them would have taken the easier route.

3. They drop the fixed mindset

When they feel that their game isn't tops, they don't just sit and accept the status quo. They take steps to make progress. A Fixed Mindset dictates that things won't change no matter the effort. A Growth Mindset, on the other hand, says that you CAN initiate change through effort, hard work, accepting feedback, and implementing strategies. To them, it all boils down to empowering beliefs. Believe you can, and you will.

4. They're willing to fail

You might be surprised to hear that the most successful people on the planet aren't the ones who never failed. They're the ones who have failed the most! The fear of failure can be paralysing – so much so that some entrepreneurs fail because they fear to start a new endeavour in the first place. *"Pain is inevitable. Suffering is optional."*, says the Dalai Lama. Successful people struggle (they struggle a lot!), but they don't think of it as suffering because they know that they are on track to pursuing a goal. Successful people agree that tough times are inevitable.

5. They seek the best, not perfection

The pursuit of perfection is strongly connected to stress, anxiety, and burnout. Successful people have lofty goals, but they are also realistic. They know that progress is progress … and they never stop pursuing it.

6. They take risks

Former Yahoo! CEO Marissa Meyer says that she would always do something she was "a little ready NOT to do." It was how she grew. That moment of not being sure that she could push her through those difficult moments was when she would have a breakthrough. Truly, growth and comfort don't co-exist, says Ginni Rometty, CEO IBM. These women know that success comes to those who go out on a limb.

7. They always invest in themselves

Books, education, courses, family, business relations … successful people enrich themselves through continuous improvement, learning, and self-education. Warren Buffet is a huge advocate for learning. To him, the most important investment one can make is in oneself. Warren Buffet began with $100 and turned it into $30 billion – which goes to show that it isn't how much money you have, but the knowledge you have.

Bonus tip: is to ask for help, even if you don't think you need it.

How often have you said, "I can figure this out; I want to do it myself?" What you really mean is "I don't want to accept help, because that means you are smarter than me. Because I have no self-esteem, I need to act like I know what to do all the time." Accepting help is okay – it doesn't mean you have to take all of the advice, but at least listen to others to see if what they say is helpful. Whoever can support you or show you the way doesn't matter. The end result is the only thing that matters.

A good reaction is, "If you can teach me how to do something easier, better or quicker, then I would like to learn from you." It's not because you are dumb when you can't figure out how to get what you want. It's because you are not trained to see beyond your present consciousness level. There is a tendency in the industry to lock up conventional approaches. "This is how we always have done it." We blind ourselves to the way it could be when we use that kind of thought and hang on to the way it was.

For further resources, courses and coaching please visit www.mindsetmastership.com

Chapter 4: To Gain Achievements, Success is Mandatory

"There are two types of people who will tell you that you cannot make a difference in this world: those who are afraid to try and those who are afraid you will succeed." -Ray Goforth

Introduction

There is no description of failure. Success can't be described either. Some people feel they are successful with luxury cars and wealth, while others flourish with their loved ones. You need to have your own definition of success. If you already have skills and a talent, harness that energy, and learn to develop it.

4.1. Techniques of Success

Commitment is the first necessity; commitments have to be made in life to achieve anything. Commitment and positive power clarify your goals. More importantly, it motivates you to succeed. You need to know how important it to show full commitment to your goals. How far you can go to reach your goals must be discovered.

Don't think about the outcomes; concentrate on learning. Insecurity about the outcomes makes it difficult for you to achieve your goals. Your personal life is also being obstructed. Your strengths are the key to success.

Analyse how you do a job and identify where changes are needed. Through discovery and innovation, don't hesitate to make adjustments. You are inspired to achieve your goals. If you are a student, you may feel unmotivated because your results may be poor, or you feel your job prospects are limited. Don't fret - seek assistance. You can find help online these days. It reduces pressure and lets you focus on learning more.

You should believe in the power of positivity and believe your journey is enjoyable. You have to take in all your life experiences. You will lose perspective if you begin to worry too much about the problems you encounter on the journey. It will stop you from advancing, and you may not succeed.

You get two kinds of thoughts in your mind – positive or negative. These two thoughts affect your emotions and perceptions. You have the option to choose one of these two. Positive thoughts are the better choice. They will allow you to work effectively and will also keep your morale up.

In life, imagination is key to feeling happy and generating energy. At times, using the power of creative thoughts can often be the key to victory. You have good feelings and think it's all going to happen. But if you face life's difficulties, you reduce positive energy and then imagination becomes charged with negative thoughts.

Therefore, wash the negativity away with optimistic thinking any time you imagine something unwanted. Try to understand how you will feel after your goals have been achieved. Imagine how thrilling your successful journey will be. The power of positivity and creativity will help you keep your dreams alive.

There are two types of people. The first type sits back and waits for openings, and the second type pushes themselves, takes responsibility and does things.

Don't hate the obstacles; you want to test yourself. The challenges are mostly successful. So, if the obstacles you face are the key to success, what are you waiting for? What do you expect? Figure out what frightens you on your way to your goals and be ready to face these challenges and succeed.

Avoid distractions around you. It may be difficult to study if your place of study is continuously noisy. If you receive regular Facebook or other social media updates, you may not concentrate on your work. It is, therefore, a must for you to avoid such distractions when carrying out any mission. Focus on the things that are most essential. This helps you to do your work successfully.

It's good to take the advice of others and then do things independently. Relying on others for everything is not ideal. Therefore, you should believe in constructive power and try working on all ventures independently. You should also accept some of your friends' support or advice if they have time.

Plan and check your progress periodically. If you don't know the way, you can't reach your target. Preparing the way to success allows you to explore. This lets you know what you're going to do and how you are going to do it. This is your achievement in preparation.

In addition, you will periodically check each job. During your analysis, you will take a critical approach. Your vulnerable points must be identified. It's also a must to find ways to strengthen your weaknesses.

4.2. How to Make Your Day Productive

Now you know that positivity is the key to success and the best approach. Another important thing is to make your day productive. Therefore, let's see some tips that can help you. Beginning in the morning, get up early, have a drink and a healthy breakfast, and go for a walk. This is how many successful people start their day. Next, when you go to work; identify the main tasks that you have to complete. The tasks must be prioritized and attempted in the first part of the day.

The first half of the day is fresh for tackling challenging tasks. However, some people do more than one job at a time or multitask; an ability few people have. Nevertheless, research has shown that attempting multiple tasks affect the quality of work. Therefore, one job at a time is encouraged. That is another major factor for success.

Many people spend hours working on their jobs. Learn to manage your time. The effect of overworking is burnout or exhaustion. Some people take a number of breaks when carrying out a job that they cannot manage. You must balance work with breaks, and work with determination and confidence in the power of positivity. But don't think of taking long breaks - the duration of the breaks must be managed.

Don't forget to test yourself and check your own performance throughout the day. No matter the success of your day, self-assessment is important. Any mistakes you made throughout a mission must be identified. You should know where you have done wrong.

A positive attitude is always related to success. Positivity lets you discover immense possibilities and keeps you both confident and motivated. It is, therefore, easy to succeed if you believe in positive power. You can build a positive attitude more quickly than you can imagine. Positive thoughts do not allow your mind to have any doubts.

You will see amazing changes all around you when you learn how to think positively. In reality, the brain begins to pump in free-flowing, feel-good hormones called endorphins, making you feel lighter and more relaxed. You will also notice a huge increase in confidence and will feel more capable than ever before. Your comfort zone of taking up new tasks and challenges will be high.

You will easily unlock your brakes and witness development as you never dreamed by reducing your self-restraining beliefs. Ultimately, through the use of the power of positive thinking, you will change your entire life.

4.3. The Initiation of Success

Since the beginning of time, all great teachers have aimed to make us aware that we continue building our own reality. Most importantly, we are responsible for everything in our lives, which means the good, the bad and the ugly.

We still look outside of ourselves for the answer if we assume that we are being harmed. We must first look within ourselves to get accurate answers to our issues so that we can see people and events in a new way. The outside world is a mirror of our inner world in many ways. You've got to know that. Who did not give this question any consideration? How many troubled people do you know? Until we look beyond ourselves to find the answer, no commitment, no desire, no encouragement or motivation can fix our problems.

Chapter 5: Factors Governing Mindset

"The mind is just like a muscle - the more you exercise it, the stronger it gets and the more it can expand."- Idowu Koyenikan

---

5.1. Law of Attraction

Like all natural laws, the law of attraction functions with statistical precision. It's neutral and impersonal, so it works if you want it to. It doesn't have anything to do with your temperament, religious beliefs, morals or your wealth status.

The Law of Attraction is as accurate as the Law of Gravity - an irrefutable law. No one understood gravity before the law of gravity was known, and yet it still influenced everyone. The Law of Attraction is similar. Many people don't understand the mechanics, but everyone knows it works. Just like you don't need to understand how the Law of Gravity works in order to stop you from floating into space, you don't need to understand the mechanics of how the Law of Attraction functions in your life.

You may not have known this, but you are drawn to everything you encounter in your life. Maybe that's not good news if your life hasn't been going as you want. And since most of us are unhappy with what we have produced in our lives, we've become masters of attracting an influx of negative circumstances.

You need to become aware of the unconscious patterns of thought that control our lives, as we attract what we envision. The primary role of the subconscious mind is to be directed by the conscious mind. This is achieved by "proving" that anything the conscious mind thinks is real. So, if you believe that you can't do something or can't have what you want, the subconscious creates circumstances to find proof that you are 'right.'

The world around you is not altered by your subconscious. It only filters the data you provide to support the image you have in mind. When, for instance, you think business is bad, or your company has no new opportunities, your subconscious can neglect potential ways of improving your business. It only suggests problems that affirm your belief that things are bad, or that new opportunities do not exist. You will bring nothing more to yourself than things which are compatible with your deepest inner convictions. You will feel powerless to change your life for the better if you do not understand that you build your reality with your thoughts. Instead, you will believe that you are a victim of other people, situations and circumstances.

If you consider yourself to be powerless, you must look for something or someone outside of yourself to fulfil your needs. Through clear thinking, you will realise that you can give yourself what you want, and you can create everything that you want.

5.2. Have Faith in your Creative Power

You must trust the Power within you to build what you want. Now, when you're told to trust the Power inside yourself, you might say, "But, see the poverty. See the illnesses, the conflict and the violence in the world. If this "Power" existed, why would any of these things happen?"

We can use this power to create everything in our lives that we want. Everything comes from our thoughts. In other words, it's done to you as you think, not as you want. Now, what would you do if you wanted more power? You would generate less resistance to handle the additional power flow.

You and I are imaginative people, and we are always able to build more. We create, knowingly or unconsciously all the time. By

76

realising who we are, we can start moving our creation from the unconscious to the conscious through the cycle of expanding the energy inside.

5.3. Your Unlimited Power

Controlling your thoughts is in your power. A distracted mind can lead you to sickness, misery, scarcity and restriction instead of towards wealth, health and achievement. We are creating from our unconscious if we do not make our lives the way we want them to be. But as life is consciousness, the most important task that we have is to achieve the highest knowledge. We can do it, even if our pride is challenged by looking at the situation of our lives and questioning our beliefs.

Chapter 6: Know the Truth about Yourself

"If you tell the truth, you don't have to remember anything." - Mark Twain

---

You must have a basic understanding of who you are if you want to have control over your life. The key to a successful life is creating your own self-image. This image is compatible with your attitude, thoughts, behaviours and even your skills. Be the type of person you claim to be. False identities can harden your self-image. Either you are happy and successful with yourself, or you oppress your life.

The circumstances that shaped your self-image may have been a misunderstanding or blown out of proportion, but they are real for you. Once you know why you feel a certain way, your feelings are valid. You can believe something is true even if it's not true.

You have to know who you are as a person, and what you are not. Who we are could be morally perfect, but what we do is not always ideal. If we don't consider ourselves spiritually perfect, our actions will be less than perfect.

6.1. Ego

Your ego fools you and convinces you of what is untrue. It wants you to look down upon yourself. It makes you identify with all that you are not. It would like you to criticise, denounce and blame yourself for not meeting your goals and other expectations. You must know you are being fooled by your ego. It doesn't usually speak the truth.

Note, one of the most important steps to changing your life is to know that you are spiritually complete and good no matter what you want to be or have. To neutralise your ego, you must love yourself unconditionally.

You have to realise that life is about mindfulness. What you believe to be reality is your own truth. When your habits of thought say, "I cannot have this or that, I don't deserve it, I am a bad person," and so forth, you keep creating circumstances that limit your opportunities.

The bottom line is this: you must accept that you are worthy and deserving of yourself.
The solution is for you to develop unconditional love. This is the only way you can be at a safer place.

6.2. You Create Yourself

You have built yourself whether or not you know it. You borrowed, imitated or made yourself all the traits of character, mannerisms, ways of speaking, facial expressions, gestures and even ways of thinking and believing. You may have been influenced by your mother, a favourite teacher, a relative, or a character in a book or film. Perhaps you borrowed a trait that you don't like. For example, perhaps you imitate traits from a person who made you feel nervous or scared. Imitating that person might help you feel less fearful and intimidated.

6.3. Never Belittle Yourself

It is essential to take a look at your personality. Perhaps if you are an imitator, you have difficulty identifying yourself. Giving up on this is not unusual. It might help to understand that no one can build themselves from scratch.

Even if you may have built your personality by imitation, you are not a fraud. Nobody else has ever had the exact same mix of traits as you. Consider this: there are only twelve musical notes, and yet several hundred thousand unique and beautiful combinations are made.

Everything depends on how these combinations are organised. Imitating parts of a personality doesn't make you any less special than someone else. The beautiful thing about this is that you can change it anytime because YOU put it together from scratch. You are never trapped. You are never stuck. It's okay if you find you're not the person you thought you were. Consider it the start of something new.

6.4. Self-Acceptance is Freedom

The ego can cause you to feel that you are incompetent, inadequate, dangerous, dumb, poor, bad and unworthy. This can reduce your self-confidence and produce a poor self-image. Unless you make a conscious decision to change your thinking patterns, you will continue to have poor self-esteem and poor self-image. You must embrace yourself to love yourself. You can only start loving others when you respect yourself.

Some people say that you ought to forget about yourself and just love others. Well, that's not how it works. The fact is, you have to recognise yourself with all your errors — all your so-called sins, every time you looked like a follower, and every time you did wrong.

The way you see yourself influences your actions and determines your performance. No matter how hard you try, someone will think you are doing something wrong. Remember this: in someone's eyes, you will always be a failure. You can't win everybody over. You just can't please everyone, so you must learn to please yourself and like who you are. It is worth remembering that who you are is perfect in spirit, but what you do is not always perfect. Just know that you cannot fail as a person in your life. That's not how you are built.

Whether you blame yourself or others for the things you did or did not do, you are in pain. Suffering is a way to get down to it and allow yourself to be upset. Maybe you did not live up to a dream that you had for yourself. Maybe you didn't live up to someone else's expectations. Self-hatred is one of the main causes of self-destructive behaviour. Many of us judge ourselves by what we have or don't have, and what we have accomplished or not accomplished.

If we do not live up to the standards of our families, bosses, or peers, we might decide that we are just no good. This is referred to as self-judgment. You might judge yourself as unworthy. As soon as you're criticised for something you've done or something you haven't figured out, you feel bad. Moreover, this kind of criticism sculpts the little self-esteem you have. It's never healthy; it's damaging. Every person has moments they regret, but they must stop regretting and move on at some point.

6.5. How you Treat Yourself Forms the Basis of your Mindset

Questions to ask yourself:

-Do you like yourself?
-Do you have confidence in yourself?
-Do you deliver on your promises?
-Do you think you're a good person?
-Would you create an act to cover up who you are?
-Would you keep someone like you as a friend?

Looking at how we deal with ourselves is very important. Often, I hear people say, "I want to explore my inner-self, but I am afraid of what I will find out about myself. I am afraid of strange discoveries which I may find along the way." We're our own worst enemy most of the time.

Chapter 7: Self-Discovery

"Knowing yourself is the beginning of all wisdom." - Aristotle

---

Start your self-discovery journey right away. Nothing but good can come out of it. Understanding your fear helps to heal the fear. Don't worry if you're better or worse than other people. Try to know yourself, instead, as the type of person you are and the person you want to become.

You don't condemn a semi-finished house while it is still under construction - you just know that you need to do more work. Take this approach to yourself. Regardless of your current condition, just realise that you need more construction. Be gentle with yourself but be adamant about the required work.

Self-worth: You will never be able to love yourself if you feel your value comes from what others think.

A self-aware person understands his personality, and he knows all about those who are of the same sort. Know who you are, and you will know how many others are like you.

Do not be afraid to reveal yourself, even if what you are revealing seems like a disadvantage. Power begins when you acknowledge your weaknesses. It's always good that you know your weaknesses, no matter how difficult or shocking they may be. Keep this in mind, especially in times when you know you must give up on something but feel unable to do so. Having the courage to recognise your weaknesses helps you change yourself.

If you learn the truth about yourself and live your life as you want, many people will not approve because they are unable to go the same way as you. Should you deny your own wealth because other people are poor? Should you reject feeling well because there are millions of sick people? Look carefully into what you deny yourself and never think of yourself as "fake" because of your wishes.

We are bound to make mistakes on our path to self-discovery. You are not those so-called mistakes, flaws or sins. Make sure you differentiate who you are from what you have and do. You know that what happens in life is fleeting and will always change. You have to realise that your Higher Self is unchanging. When you identify with your temporary nature, you accept that you are what you have, and you are what you do. It may be the biggest mistake you make in your life.

As you stand on the seaside and look at boats sailing around, there is no problem as long as you just stand and watch them go through. You will only experience pain and suffering if you interact with the vessels. You might grieve when it passes by your sight if you say, "That's MY ship." You might live in fear of someone else being its captain by thinking, "I must command that ship." Likewise, if we take on passing issues as our own, we may feel responsible for errors and faults just by merely observing them.

When you begin to question your life and examine it honestly, you come to the point where you realise that the only source of authority is you. Though you might be waiting for others to tell you what you need to do, you alone know what to do. Maybe you don't want to be responsible for your own life, or you'd rather other people make decisions for you. But understand this truth: So long as you allow other people to be responsible for your future, they govern your destiny.

7.1. Change your World

It is easy to say that others are to blame for our problems, but this way of thinking binds us further because we limit our independence. We are to blame.

Again, to straighten your thinking means to separate what you have from who you are. Separate the "doer" from the "deed." In our current culture, the trick is to live but to disallow the world to live in us.

Let me ask you before I go any further: "Why do you want your world to change?" We need to improve our perspectives.

When you return to the fundamental principle of life, you realise that in the universe, nothing happens that you cannot accept deep within your consciousness. Some things have been done to you, as you believe, and these convictions are sometimes very strong. Everything takes place within our minds, even though we may not be aware of it, is in profound harmony with our experiences without it. I know it is difficult to embrace the rule because you don't want things in your life.

The reality is, however, that you are meeting a deep inner desire. Imagine an unhappy person sitting in his house, saying, "I want to change my life." Then he's as sad as he was before. He redecorates many times, but to himself, he still has no sense of change.

Do you know people who believe their happiness will improve by altering their outer landscape? Where did that error come from? How can they correct themselves?

You can discover what is happening if you are fully honest with yourself and take a good look at what is happening in your life. This process of self-evaluation is an excellent way to find yourself if you no longer know what to do.

The truth is, you are not what you have, and you are not what you do. Your spiritual completion, completeness and perfection are in direct proportion to your ability to accept this reality about yourself.

7.2. Identify your Goals

"Setup the mind for the best," this will be discussed in depth later. But, for now, you only need to realise that looking at a photo isn't like watching a film. If the picture cannot be identified, you won't remember it because the image is not registered in the subconscious level.

In your image, you will "shadow" yourself. The final result is intentional reinforcement or self-talk, paired with visualisation. If we keep visualising it again and again, our subconscious will agree that it's real for us very soon.

In the beginning, there is tension between where you are or what you have and what you implicitly embrace. Nevertheless, one of the main functions of the unconscious is to solve conflicts between what we think about and what we live by. And because our subconscious is creative, what we think of and visualise begins to be created.

First of all, you need to change your image. Real growth and improvement start from within. Your comfort zone will naturally grow, and you will act accordingly to your new truth or religion.

How do you know what your self-image is? Accept your actions, attitudes and results. Also, ask yourself, "What do I expect of myself? Where do I feel out of place?" You will unconsciously do things to let yourself be lost if you see yourself as poor. What do you think you say to yourself when you lose? "I've never got money." This reinforces your image, which triggers your self-talk again, which enhances the picture, and thus continues. "I'm like that," "I'm still lost," "I never have cash."

People feel oppressed without money, but what they don't understand is that they live a self-fulfilling prophecy. This is why wealthy people get wealthier and the poor stay poor. It doesn't have anything to do with money.

Those with winning self-images do winning things. They don't accept losing as their destiny if they lose occasionally. You know it's not natural for you to lose. You deny it by saying, "That wasn't like me" or "This doesn't happen to me."

7.3. Your Attitude Affects your Success

Understanding the difference between success and failure is crucial. Attitudes are prevailing convictions. The assessment of an attitude is always objective. Once you have set a goal, an attitude can either help you achieve it or prevent you from reaching your target.

People are often looking for problems or ways to avoid problems because of the attitudes they created. Most of these attitudes were unintentionally created.

If you have an attitude that causes you to avoid situations, you can make a conscious decision to change. All you have to do is make a new statement, visualise the end result, and re-imagine yourself as a person with the attitude you desire. You can see yourself looking for a particular action in daily life, or in some cases avoid, if you choose.

You shall either remain where you are or persuade yourself that it is in your best interest to change with deliberate intention. If you choose to change, you must imagine your new belief. Constructive self-talk and imagination help you evolve without anxiety, pressure and negative feedback in a controlled way.

People have a certain self-image for different aspects of their lives. My subconscious must ensure that I always do what is real. My self-image influences my success in how I behave or act.

We want to focus on our self-image rather than relying on our actions. How are we doing? We begin to regulate our self-talk so that when our behaviour becomes different than how we want it to be, we will say to ourselves, "That is not how I am. That's not like me." Our images are controlled by direct self-talk.
We can imagine a new behaviour, even if it is the opposite of our attitude or actions right now. Make sure the behaviour is tested to achieve the desired end result. When the picture you imagine changes, the output will change as well.

In relation to the goal, our subconscious imaginative process knows precisely where we are in time and place. This stimulates creative energy and drives people to look at material things, new books, seminars or anything else to create our images. But the first picture has to come. Without an image, we can't begin.

This unconscious imaginative process gives you a strategy to use your creative skills. It is essential to control what you are picturing. It needs to be established clearly and explicitly. What is it? How is it? You can't have it if you can't describe it.

7.4. Never Force Change – That is failure

"I must lose weight" "I must work harder." That very pressure is unconsciously working against the end results you seek. The greatest pit that we fall into is forcing change, like trying to control ourselves and telling ourselves, "I must do this."

If you think you have to do something, it's your job to say, "No, you don't have to do anything." And with clever diversion, delay, or any way you can, you find a way to stop it. If you think, 'I must,' then you can say, 'But I would rather do something else.' The harder you try to do something, the more you work against your artistic subconscious.

I have strength in me that most people have given up, because I know I can make a difference, because it's my idea to be like that. I should stop saying "I have to," and say "I can." I will be as my imagination tells me, I can and will step constructively towards that end result with exciting magnetic energy and drive. I know that I am a self-made individual, that both succeeds and fails, and that this success or failure is my power. You become a powerful person when you rely on commitments to yourself and others. You are just as strong as your word.

When you give your word to other people that you will be somewhere at a certain time, you have to be able to follow through, because every time you don't hold your word, you lose control. You need to be able to depend on yourself to do what you say you will do.

Keep your mind open about what you want and don't want to do. Do not spend time thinking about what you are trying to avoid. Go towards what you want rather than trying to get away from what you don't want. Every moment is a new start. High-performing successful people look at what they want and work toward the final result. So, what do you want? That's what you need to know. Does it make you happy? Why are you going to work? Why should you go to school? Why do you get involved? For yourself, what do YOU want?

When you do what you like to do – purposefully – you will draw in people and situations that are needed to help you serve your mission. Understand, you're drawn to what you believe and visualise. Start by understanding where you want to go and start talking about it with yourself.

Chapter 8: Seeing is Believing

"Faith is to believe what you do not see; the reward of this faith is to see what you believe." -
Saint Augustine

There is a general belief that "If I see it, it is true." We've also learned that people do not always adhere to the facts, but to their understanding of the truth.

8.1. Success Suffers a Setback due to Perception of Reality

People who have to see things before they can believe in them, or who need specific advice before they take a risk, probably find growing and changing to be difficult. They spend most of their lives waiting for something instead of doing it.

Our perception of reality is limited in the use of our imagination. We have to take a good look to see if our perception of reality is perhaps skewed or distorted in order to change it.

Even though we are all in the same universe, we interpret what we see differently.

All our decisions and actions are based on our awareness at any given moment. To be all that we can potentially be, our awareness or our perception of reality must constantly be changed and expanded.

A misperception of the majority of people is that "seeing is believing." But the fact is, just because we can't see something, doesn't mean it isn't there. The first thing that you have to ask yourself is, what is important or valuable to me? What am I looking for, and what are the results I want? You can't achieve goals until you understand exactly what you want. By knowing exactly what you want - what kind of home, job, vehicle, income, or, relationships; you increase your knowledge of useful resources and data that will help you achieve your target.

Naturally, our brain filters out knowledge which is of no interest to us or threatens our safety. The knowledge will start to flow through once we decide what we want. Remember, it doesn't mean it doesn't exist because we can't see it. It only means that we block information that we currently don't care about.

This is a necessary shielding mechanism that prevents us from becoming crazy. This mechanism can, however, restrict our opportunities if left unchecked.

A great deal of information is available at any given time to help you build what you want. Nonetheless, most people try to solve problems without deciding precisely what they want to achieve.

8.2. Focusing on the End Result

What do you need to know to get the end result you want? Here's an example of focusing on the end result: suppose you are interested in a specific car. Your mind is made up; you plan to buy no other car. Then everywhere you look, you see this car. Why does this happen? It's because your mind is now set on this particular brand.

This method can be used to find the customers, jobs, businesses or individuals you want to engage with. As soon as you know who or what you are looking for, you will find them/it. If you don't know what you are searching for, you won't find it.

8.3. Think Outside your Limitations

We don't see possibilities because we restrict the way we think. We have to be prepared to think outside our limits. If we encounter opposing thoughts, views or behaviours at the same time, we sometimes feel emotionally uncomfortable. Once anxiety comes in, we rationalise very quickly why we should stop, give up, or why we can't do something. Generally, a change in attitude is necessary to reduce the anxiety caused by the change.

Rationalisation is the most common way of alleviating disputes. Rationalisation is what people use when they try to explain why they do what they do. To avoid looking foolish, a person gathers information that supports their opinion or their behaviour. For example, there is a tendency to only see the good features of a person and ignore any of the negative characteristics.

Ironically, we block knowledge that may be useful for rational decisions, and ultimately blind ourselves from other alternatives. We feel the need to try and prove that we are correct. You can use your subconscious to help you find ideas and responses, but you use the same subconscious to justify why it cannot be achieved. You always have the choice, and you always have the option.

8.4. What We Think, We Attract

Sometimes you don't feel like doing or getting what you really want. The bigger your self-worth, the greater your interest, the more opportunities and the more risks you will take. An honest self-worth person says, "I can do everything I want to do."

Chapter 9: Create your Own Story

"Most of us have only one story to tell. I don't mean that only one thing happens to us in our lives: there are countless events, which we turn into countless stories. But there's only one that matters, only one finally worth telling."
- Julian Barnes

Every human being has an inherent desire to achieve their potential. Three principal convictions in life keep us from being happy and satisfied: The first is: what I have is not better than what others have. The grass is always greener on the other side. The second belief is that it is easier to have more: more would be better regardless of how much I have. The third conviction is: I'll be happy if I get what I want. Is that really true?

9.1. Is your life about Problems or Solutions?

The success ethic described simply says, "When you get what you want, you're going to be happy." It's based on the theory that one day we'll be happy if we work harder and solve every problem in our lives.

All the problems you have to solve and how hard you have to work are the first things many of us think about when we get up in the morning. We were trained to think about what is not, what should be, what shouldn't be, and how we should fix or change a situation. But if you look honestly into your life, solving problems, working hard, and having all of the things you want will not radically change the quality of your life. Indeed, focusing on these areas has probably diminished the fun and excitement of living your best life.

Assume your life will be changed by a new job. You've got a new job, and quite quickly it's the same old thing; you're dealing with taking responsibility, meeting deadlines and working with others who are not so well-informed. You will then realise that this new job didn't make a big difference in how you feel, so something else needs to be found to satisfy you.

Perhaps you think your life will improve with a new mate, a new home, a baby, or more money. You might get those things eventually, but still aren't happy.

The explanation is clear. Nothing else will ever make us happy because happiness is an internal experience. It begins by being.

Our intentions are vibrations setting the universe in motion

Did you ever wonder why New Year resolutions do not work? What happens is that we are always saying things like "I will no longer eat candy," "I will stop screaming at the boys," "I will stop eating too much." But remember that New Year resolutions weren't about what you wanted. It's a kind of negative self-talk about what you don't want, rather than a picture of what you do want.

Setting objectives is an important factor that will determine your success or failure. Have you ever been on a business trip without at least knowing where you were going?

Have you ever played tennis without knowing where the courtyard was?

Would you leave to go shopping without having any idea of how to get there?

Have you ever been on holiday without realising where you were going?

"I want to be spontaneous. I want to be free to change my mind." Well, sometimes we falsely believe that freedom means avoiding commitment. Ultimately, our capacity to make decisions and commitments is true freedom. Our question is "What do I really want?" Start from a place where you know what you want on some level. You will decide at some point. Keep this in mind - if you don't know what you want, then someone else is going to choose for you. It won't end up being what you really want because it was someone else's decision.

Chapter 10: Success, Mindset and Law of Attraction

"Try not to become a man of success. Rather become a man of value." - Albert Einstein

---

"The true measure of success is how many times you can bounce back from failure." - Stephen Richards

---

Your way of thinking and spirituality influences your life, from how you think and feel about what you are doing and how you respond to the world around you.

Here are eight powerful ways to improve your thoughts:

- Adjust your negative self-talk to a self-empowering talk. It sounds cliché, but it works to say, "I can do it," or "I got this." The mind will then open up new ways of thinking to help achieve your goal.

- Adjust your language: To promote a positive attitude, avoid phrases such as "I'm always like that," or "I always do that." Make it a habit, instead of moaning about your problems, to talk about things that go well in your life.

- Find out what mindset you need to achieve a goal and ask, "What thinking do I need to accomplish that goal?" and "what is the thought of people who succeeded in this?"

- Identify and conquer your personal limiting beliefs that keep you from achieving your full potential of mind.

- To grasp and change your ideas, read the books about the workings of the mind and brain. Learn through online courses, activities and training from experts in learning. Here are some of my favourite mental resources: Carol Dweck's insight into the growth mentality, everything from Gabrielle Bernstein.

- You want to boost your money & success? Surround yourself with people who display positive attitudes. Start a social circle with people who are doing what you want to be doing. When you see what is effective for other people, it is easier to adjust to a new way of thinking.

- Create new ways to help change your thinking - incorporate effective ways of thinking that can change your mind and strengthen your thought. Actively search for opportunities that can help you grow and learn.

- Step out of your comfort zone: You have no choice but to stand up for this occasion and refine your ideas. When you encounter circumstances that threaten you. It's survival.

10.1. Manifesting Success Using the Law of Attraction

Since "The Secret" became popular, the Law of Attraction has become a big phrase. I strongly believe in the power of attraction. Our thoughts generate a flow of energy, and this energy is identical to our thoughts. So, if you concentrate on how much your day sucks, guess what? Crappier experiences will draw you in.

You'll have a much more positive experience and pull positive things into your life if you're in a headspace reflecting on everything that you're thankful for during your day.

How do you carry this willing abundance into your life? Take the following steps:

- Be very specific about what you want to put into your life. If you want a new job, make a list of everything you need to be happy with the job.

- Write your goals down. Research has revealed that you can accomplish your goals 42 per cent more when they are written down. Most specifically, focus on how you will understand all of these things.

- Imagine that you already have what you want. Schedule time to sit every day and envision your ideal feelings. Consider this like your daily meditation, where you can already see yourself with what you want. Maybe imagine yourself in a new office, running your own business, or driving that new car. The more you envision, the more you will truly believe it's on your way.

- Clear any mental blocks. You can tell the world all day long what you want, but if you think you are not worthy or good enough to receive what you envision, you're going to remain wherever you are.

- Have patience. Trying to quickly manipulate and force things to happen is just a way to mess up what the universe tries to do. Make sure you take steps every day to get your goals forward but know that nothing is in a hurry.

10.2. Achieve your Financial Desires

I am sure you have heard the saying that "the rich get richer and the poor get poorer." Those who are wealthy always talk about money. Those who experience poverty constantly think of misery, so it becomes a promise of self-fulfilment. The economy, recession, unemployment, interest rates or jobs have nothing to do with our success. It's because rather than focusing on what we want, we're focused on what we don't want.

The reality is that we are the makers of our own financial state. We have either sufficient or insufficient responsibilities. We must recognise this obligation before a change can be made. We reflect our negative thoughts if we feel financially trapped.

Our culture is dominated by thoughts about money and they can be pleasant or disturbing. Money cannot make you happy, but many things that make you unhappy can be done away with. Cash, whether you like it or not, will always be an important part of your life. Wealth decides the quality of your life in most situations because money gives you independence. You can either bear the agony of financial problems or use your power to solve these problems as a Deliberate Creator.

All too many people just survive - they live from paycheck to paycheck. The biggest cause of stress for the majority of adults is money problems. Because money problems can harm our wellbeing, disrupt our personal relationships, our jobs and our happiness, it should be at the top of our list to build financial stability and wealth.

We must clear up our old ideas, values and principles that prohibit us from living with wealth. This can include removing our incorrect convictions; money is tight, jobs are scarce, the economic situation isn't good for businesses, it's hard to become wealthy, or that maybe we don't deserve to be rich. Instead of the illusions we have, we need to fill our consciousness with the facts. We will ultimately affirm our own reality.

We can change our reality using statements like:

- I want to learn how to be rich.
- I have decided to gain riches.
- The sales are greater than the outflow, I get to pick.
- I allow myself to enjoy the money.
- I agree to alleviate my reluctance to be rich.
- I accept the money has just come into my life.
- I'm rich in dollars.

10.3. Create Wealth with Imagination

We always create from our imagination, but we don't understand how. We use the past to create the future and the present. Use your imagination and visualisations to create how you would like to build your life. Don't imagine it the way it was. If you do, the limitations of your past will form your future.

We must also contribute and share what we have with others. Our knowledge of our prosperity is growing each time we consider the resources we think we already have. When we increase our knowledge of our resources, our lives become more plentiful.

10.4. Be grateful – that's Being Positive

Recognise and be grateful for what you already have. Love what you have at the moment, no matter how little it seems when compared to what other people have. Instead of complaining, just appreciate what you have now. The old saying goes, "I cried because I didn't have a pair of shoes until I met a man with no feet."

Build an "attitude of thankfulness" for anything you have now and see how it will grow and grow. Buy and retain the 'Universal Bank ' definition. Each time you pay a deposit at the Universal Bank and don't see a return immediately, realise that at least 138 times you made your deposit in interest. Everything you give out must return to you.

Don't make the mistake of trying to decide when and how your goodwill returns to you, but know that your goodwill comes to you in countless ways if you deposit in the Universal Bank. Often your abundance is quite easy to manifest. Occasionally, in unexpected ways, the goodwill comes to you. Know that it's there.

Chapter 11: Words that Create Results at a Faster Pace

"Words can be like X-rays if you use them properly, they'll go through anything. You read, and you're pierced." - Aldous Huxley

---

11.1. Your Conscious Mind Creates Result

The purpose of this exercise is to replace a set of false beliefs with facts. The unconscious mind wants to reflect on what was offered. The mind and the unconscious mind are called the synthesis of consciousness.

In the end, all we live with is the result of a cause that we have begun. Action and reaction, sowing and harvesting are always present. The value of consciousness must be acknowledged. Techniques can always be taught, but a knowledge of good thinking must be established.

I gave a sales management course to a company in a big city. I explained at the beginning that I would not be teaching them marketing mechanics. They had taken a number of courses. I said I would advise them to build a model of consciousness to establish an inner action or a mental strategy that would allow them to effortlessly sell without being deceptive. A few weeks after the end of the course, the company I was working with announced a 40-percent increase in sales and a significant increase in production for all those involved. They agreed that this kind of training was most helpful because they learned to deal with cause rather than effect.

An example would be if you stood at your front door and looked at the house number directly across the street. You can see that the number on the house is very distinctive when you concentrate on it. But you could be aware of other things on either side of the house even if you look at it without moving your eyes. The other items get more complicated as they move to the right or left of the amount of the house that is the subject. Let's look at how it applies to the cycle of learning. Your core awareness and marginal awareness are like your core vision and marginal sight. There are things you are painfully aware of in your consciousness.

This is your dominant thought. There are things that you are vaguely aware of in your limited consciousness. The marginal thoughts do not control your behaviour, even if they are negative. Your core consciousness or your dominant thoughts govern your actions and your life. You tend to attract the things you love, fear, or constantly expect, that is, the things you hold in your central consciousness.

Anything that prevents my wish from coming to fruition I am willing to give up. I am encouraged and compelled to take steps to foster this intention in all respects. And so it is.

This method is deliberately designed to produce the best results because it is based on the Creative Theory of the mind. Take the time to use it and your ability to produce performance will be increased. You will become more and more aware of the power of your word.

Chapter 12: Think Positive, Identify Your Problems and Achieve Success

---

"Instead of worrying about what you cannot control, shift your energy to what you can create."
- Roy T. Bennett

Don't be afraid if you don't know what to do. You will start to know what to do when you stop resisting the unknown. Search for your own solution whenever you have a problem or a crisis. Don't tell others about it. Through spreading it around, you dilute the severity of the issue, and you dilute the strength and awareness to eradicate it.

The next time you're in a stressful situation, do something completely new. Remember how your mind anxiously seeks an answer, relief and reassurance in the first place. Do something else, and you will be surprised by the new solutions that your intuition will show.

12.1. Identify the Problem and its Solution to Bring about the Change

Do not attempt to solve problems using your memories or previous experiences. You've attempted to solve the problem before by using outdated logic and reasoning. If you knew how to solve the problem already it would have been solved!

When a person says he or she is having a problem, it usually involves a deeper problem. The deeper issue is rarely mentioned, partly because they don't know and partly because they don't agree.

A dilemma cannot be solved if the mind is panicky. It usually turns to the wrong solution, and we continue to go in circles. If you are not in a panic to find a solution, you will be shown the right one. You can move the needle in a variety of wrong directions by shaking a compass. The arrow settles down to the correct and normal direction when you stop moving it around. This is an excellent lesson in solving problems.

You might say, "I understand, but in my case it is different. They intensified my grief. They did it to me." Unfortunately, you give up the power to change if you keep blaming others. Responsibility for the quality of your life is yours.

12.2. Self-reliance over Emotional Dependency

Instead of self-reliance, most of us practice mental dependency. "If you agree with me, and if I am able to duplicate your beliefs and values, I will gain your approval." The decision we make is, "You take care of me, you nurture me, and I will do what you want." It is a terrifying sense to be in a place where you know that your life is dependent on the good nature of another person.

The need to be right and the need to get validation results in psychological dependence. It stems from our need to be emotionally dependent so that we feel loved and cared for. This finding is important since it means that nothing else can give you true self-worth beyond yourself.

Your life is for no one but you, except you give away your power. People will try to control your life when you give your power away. You will be convinced of their knowledge.

When we want something from another person, like love, security, approval, recognition or agreement; tension arises. The expectation is that this individual will accomplish our needs for us.

The secret for a successful life is to get to know yourself. You don't have to look for love from others when you learn to love yourself. You can be more caring instead of looking for love. You can't be taken advantage of if you don't expect anything, because there is no way that anyone can manipulate you. Some people will have difficulties with you if you do not want anything from them, because they cannot control you. But this is the real way of self-reliance and psychological independence.

Adjustment of the Mental State

Most studies show that no one is too old or too young for their views, ideas, principles and pictures to change. You can actually change anything very easily about yourself. You just have to give up the illusion that it takes a long time to change.

Most of us value our television sets differently than our own views.

If our TV needs to be adjusted, we adjust it to make a clearer view. Most of us require daily change and reorganisation. This is what a creative person has to do occasionally. You can tell a person a hundred times that he has to change his views, but until that person tells himself the same thing, nothing will happen.

Be mindful if you have anxiety. Don't run away from it. We are most likely to ignore or suppress this sensation. It can be reduced to manageable proportions if you stop running away from it and face it.

Courage is merely the will to be afraid and to act

There is a line between fear and excitement. You will drive anxiety over the line to excitement if you don't allow the anxiety to stop you. But don't wait until fear becomes panic. You will be very rewarded if you have the confidence to accept your fear, rather than fleeing. It will open up new possibilities and resources for you to share your unlimited potential.

12.3. Say No to Fear of Uncertainty

Don't be afraid of fear. You can have 1,000 fears or not a single fear. You will be open to new ideas, which greatly improves your life when you give up your fear of uncertainty.

12.4. Staying Focused, Knowing your Desire – Path of Success

Do you say, "It's a wonderful day, and I feel great?" Attitudes and conviction have everything to do with it.

They say, "I tried. Heaven knows I tried! But why is something that I'm doing failing?" And then they think," I'm going to try again," but that isn't working either. Why does it not work?

It does not work because the condition of faith has not been established, which will enable them to go where they want to go. They don't trust where they were going. Rather, they concentrate on where they don't want to go. This brings us to a major question: What is your ultimate goal? What do you really want?

Now, pause for a minute. There is no way for you to continue your journey if you cannot answer this question.

The solution is to find out exactly what you want and what you want to do.

How would you explain what your life is like? What are you interested in? If you can answer this honestly, then you're at a good start. Don't put yourself down if the life you really want hasn't been lived. Everything you have done in the past has nothing to do with what you want to do now. Respect the life you led, even if you want to change it.

Someone asked me once what I felt was one of a person's most destructive behaviours. There are many ways of serious self-destruction, but I must say that blind obedience is at the height of the list. To me, it encourages people to do things without thought — the most dangerous thing in the world. In Nazi Germany, millions of Jews were killed with that mentality. The world needs people who challenge and think for themselves more than anything else.

Don't challenge your wishes. The only way you will ever learn if something is right is to experience it. You will find out in time if it is not the right thing. You can then make changes. Life is a corrective cycle. Nonetheless, many people are afraid to make mistakes and are not willing to correct them, so they never get there.

12.5. Say No to Fear of Change

Why haven't we created exactly the kind of life we want to have? We are conditioned to worry about change. We would rather be consistently miserable than take a chance for fear of losing joy and fulfilment. We are always programmed to seek safety and security, and also to fear the unknown. Decision-making teaches you something. Don't get caught in the middle of the pendulum between "yes" and "no" or swing back and forth between "yes" and "no."

Change means addressing the unfamiliar. It consists of moving from the known to the unknown and involves risk. How would you feel if you changed your job today, to one with a higher wage, more opportunities for growth, and better working conditions? You might have some doubt, fear, or insecurity about the change. Even if the shift is good, people can be nervous. It's completely normal.

12.6. Difference between Successful and Unsuccessful People

How successful people manage change is the difference between successful and unsuccessful people. Successful individuals also have anxiety, but they are not immobilised, unlike unsuccessful people.

Successful people are still nervous but turn to innovation. You may know the "Peter Principle," where each of us eventually reaches our failure point and then remains stuck because they are unable to continue. People can remain stuck because of fear of change and refusal to reassess and reprogram to adapt. The Peter Principle states we have limited capacity. But the truth is that due to our fear of change, we stop developing our abilities.

What you have been advised to do is reflect on what isn't, what ought to be, and what might have been. We are brought up with a value system that says that we should assess ourselves continuously, measure ourselves and see whether we are "good." We are judged so rigorously that, because we are afraid to make mistakes, we stop bringing results.

We were taught to be afraid of the unknown and so, instead of focusing on what is, we continue to be worried about what might happens two weeks from now. But the fact is, there will always be the unknown, no matter what you do.

Chapter 13: The Amazing 7 Growth Hacks

"Don't go through life, grow through life." - Eric
Butterworth

If you are not where you really want to be, there's likely something in the background that is holding you back. Can you imagine what it is? Hint: It has the power to transform your life completely–you have a choice. It's positive (or negative). It's the MINDSET!

Your thoughts drip into every area of your life and can change your job, your career, your mind, your relationship and your life in general. That is why, in order to shift your outlook and push you more positive towards life, I dig into my top 7 mind-set hacks.

Hack 1 - Become Aware Of Your Thoughts

Your thoughts are all about you. It is important to look closely at your feelings, as we often aren't aware of what we think. The more you watch over your emotions, the more you realise that you are fully controlled by them.

Hack 2 - Reframe Your Thoughts Using The Ctfar Model

The CTFAR Model is the idea that thoughts create feelings, feelings create your behaviours and ultimately your outcomes. You can take power back in your life by seeing the world in that way. Instead of the passenger, you are the driver of your life.

The CTFAR Model

1. **Circumstances**: are neutral.
2. **Thoughts:** are optional.
3. **Feelings**: what are the feelings associated with these thoughts?
4. **Action**: how do those feelings determines the action we take?
5. **Result**: what is the result caused by the action?

For example, you may experience a thought with mixed feelings: anger and rage generate varying feelings.

You can use the CTFAR model to create different paths, each ending with different results. By including all your path possibilities, you will also expose unwanted thought patterns. Once you decide on the one that arrives at the best outcome and brings the most joy, utilise that model.

To create your various models, use sticky notes on a wall so that you can visualise the varying thoughts and feelings. This is a very practical method you can use to adjust, thoughts, feelings and actions, giving you a clear insight into your thoughts, and the best way to proceed.

Hack 3 - Positive Affirmations

It goes without saying that if you repeat something enough, you will start to believe it.

There are so many affirmations I love to use every day, but here is one of my favourites: I control my life, my life doesn't control me. You must envision your future as you want it. By doing so, you instinctively identify with your future and get closer every day to bring it.

Hack 4 - Get Rid Of Limiting Words

The self-talk represents your values, and anything you think will ultimately become the outcome in your life. Therefore, modifying your vocabulary to match your thought is so important. I would advise you to start by eliminating specific words like "can't," "don't," "unable, "never". People who succeed are thinking, "I can do XYZ, I will do XYZ, and I'll get it done today." Remove yourself from your feelings and ask what you think. Adjust your language to support the person you want to be. Please ask yourself (see below) powerful questions that will bring you closer to your future.

Hack 5 - Ask Yourself Questions

If you ask negative questions, then negative answers will be received; but if you ask positive questions, then positive answer will be given. So, if you're wondering "Why am I always poor?" The brain will only focus on reasons that you are poor. But, when you ask, "How can I earn more money?" The brain comes with ideas on how to make more money for you. Here you can ask yourself some big questions:

- What can I do today to get me closer to my goals?
- In my business, how can I make more money?
- Who do I want to be in the future?
- How would I think, behave and feel if I was the person that I want to be?
- To achieve my goals, what do I need to know?
- What do I still don't know?
- If I could believe something, what would I believe?

Asking these questions can help you dive deeper into answers that produce the most results.

Hack 6 - Add "No Matter What" To Your Thought Process

This hack is a mentality I like to use when I'm not motivated to deal with my most difficult task. Essentially, if I have anything important to do, but I sense some pressure, I assure myself that I will achieve the mission. For instance, I would tell myself that I no matter what, I need to write 15 blog posts in a day or organise my closet. I'm a person who is going to do all I can to get what I want if I want it bad enough.

Hack 7 - Create An Alter Ego For Yourself

I like to use this hack most of all! It is based on Todd Herman's book *The Alter Ego Effect*. Do you feel like you want something in your life, but then feel like you don't? Does your own personality make you stand still in your own way and take no opportunity?

Here is a convenient way to create an alter ego. To begin with, think of the person you would like to be who has the results you want. Next, create an alter ego of the ideal person and pretend to be it until you really become it.

I have altered egos for various areas of my life, whether it is for company or health purposes. I offer myself the freedom to make myself stronger and bolder. You continue to adopt the habits and values by practising being your alter ego.

Now go back to the start of this book and utilise the bonus change hacks mentioned at the beginning. These 3 extra change hacks will help solidify your progress.

Final Thoughts

If you use these hacks, they will change your mindset from scarcity to abundance, so you can take away any restrictive confidence that holds you back and finally build the life of which you have dreamt!

I had a lot of convictions that I couldn't understand, and they kept me behind for years. I lacked the strength and insight to move forward with faith in my life until I did these activities and worked on my attitude every day. I promise you can do the same! My recommendation is to incorporate these separately, and before you know it, you will change profoundly!

Conclusion

Positive thinking is a healing agent for not just your body, but for your soul too, therefore initiating a process of self-improvement ultimately embarking on a path of success followed by achieving it. According to recent research "happy people" are more pleased with their work and show more independence.

Moreover, they perform best and receive more support from their colleagues than their less happy peers. Ultimately, the odds of positive people becoming unemployed are lower, their mentally safer, and they are likely to live longer. And the argument about happiness and jobs goes back a long way in history.

The ancient Greek philosopher Galen said that work was "nature's physician," key to the happiness of humans.

"Power Naps" can improve right-brain activities that will lead to opportunities when people are optimistic at work because they are more active and resilient. The book explicitly covered how to learn to think positively, what are the factors that govern positive thinking and how a positive mindset makes it easier to achieve a positive attitude thereby ensuring success.

Success is beyond positive thinking but definitely the outcome of it. You always start with the basics that later translate into bigger achievements. Positive thinking is the first step to any change in life. A positive attitude is achieved when even your subconscious is in harmony with your conscious state of mind with which you intentionally instil a habit of positive thinking.

All this ultimately helps you to create your own reality. When you are aware of your capabilities, only then you can subjugate all the fears of change and uncertainty. Big achievements are marked by a series of big and small mistakes. Nothing goes perfect all along the way. Accept the very essence of every successful journey and keep on the path consistently with a changing pace. As nothing is attained at a steady pace, there are highs there are lows, what matters at the end of the day is staying focused. Growth, no matter how small, is growth - and every step towards it counts. That is how you become successful with a positive mindset.

To learn more about instilling better habits see our book How To Change Habits in 30 days: 7 Hacks

To learn more about coaching and mindset training see our website: www.MindsetMastership.com

References

- Abundance Coach for Women in Business | Evelyn Lim. (2020). *7 Steps to Self-Discovery*. [online] Available at: https://www.evelynlim.com/7-steps-to-self-discovery/.

- We Wait He Works. (2020). *Believing is Seeing.* [online] Available at: https://www.beliefnet.com/columnists/wewaitheworks/2017/12/believing-is-seeing.html.

- wikiHow. (2020). *How to Be Able to Create a Story*. [online] Available at: https://www.wikihow.com/Be-Able-to-Create-a-Story.

- Jake Ducey. (2020). *Jake Ducey*. [online] Available at: https://www.jakeducey.com/blog/law-of-attraction/the-most-powerful-law-of-attraction-mindset/.

- James Clear. (2020). *How Positive Thinking Builds Skills, Boosts Health, and Improves Work*. [online] Available at: https://jamesclear.com/positive-thinking.

- OptinMonster. (2020). *The 11 Best Growth Hacking Strategies to Skyrocket Your User Base*. [online] Available at: https://optinmonster.com/growth-hacking-strategies/.

- Psychology Today. (2020). *The Truth About the Law of Attraction*. [online] Available at: https://www.psychologytoday.com/us/blog/the-blame-game/201609/the-truth-about-the-law-attraction.

- Ayan, S. (2020). *10 Things You Don't Know about Yourself*. [online] Scientific American. Available at:

https://www.scientificamerican.com/article/10-things-you-dont-know-about-yourself/.

- Sam Thomas Davies. (2020). *Book Summary: Unlimited Power by Anthony Robbins.* [online] Available at: https://www.samuelthomasdavies.com/book-summaries/self-help/unlimited-power/.

- TheJobNetwork. (2020). *9 Strategies to Make Every Day Productive.* [online] Available at: https://www.thejobnetwork.com/9-strategies-to-make-every-day-productive/.

- Points That Prove That Positive Thinking Can Lead You to Success - Thrive Global. (2019). Retrieved from https://thriveglobal.com/stories/4-points-that-prove-that-positive-thinking-can-lead- you-to-success/

- 8 Effective Ways to Upgrade Your Mindset for Success. (2019). Retrieved from https://medium.com/swlh/8-effective-ways-to-upgrade-your-mindset-for-success-e1687830f649S

- Dr. Robert Anthony, (2004). *Beyond Positive Thinking.* March 21, 2020. Available at: https://saidnazulfiqar.files.wordpress.com/2008/04/beyond-positive-thinking.pdf

- Jake Ducey. (2019). *The Most Powerful Law of Attraction Mindset.* March 18, 2020. Available at: https://www.jakeducey.com/blog/law-of-attraction/the-most-powerful-law-of-attraction-mindset/

- Farnam Street. (2016). *Carol Dweck: When a Fixed Mindset is Better than a Growth Mindset*. March 18, 2020. Available at https://fs.blog/2016/02/carol-dweck-growth/

- Alexander Clark. (2018). *Your Biggest Asset for Academic Career Success? A Growth Mindset.* March 18, 2020. Available at https://www.timeshighereducation.com/blog/your-biggest-asset-academic-career-success-growth-mindset

- Sharan B. Merriam. (2003). *Andragogy and Self-Directed Learning: Pillars of Adult Learning Theory*. March 18, 2020.

- Helen Colman. (2019). *6 Adult Learning Theories and How to Put Them Into Practice.* March 18, 2020. Available at https://www.ispringsolutions.com/blog/adult-learning-theories

- Zee. (2013). *It Doesn't Take 10,000 Hours to Learn a New Skill. It Takes 20. And Here's How...* March 18, 2020. Available at https://thenextweb.com/lifehacks/2013/10/24/doesnt-take-10000-hours-learn-skill-takes-20-heres-now/

- Develop Good Habits. (2019). *Famous Failures: 30 Stories of Successful People Who Once Failed*. March 18, 2020. Available at https://www.developgoodhabits.com/successful-people-failed/

- Connie Stemmle. (2019). *20 Growth Mindset Examples to Change Your Beliefs*. March 18, 2020. Available at https://www.developgoodhabits.com/growth-mindset-examples/

- Jennifer Gunn. (2020). *Building A Growth Mindset for Teachers*. March 18, 2020. Available at https://blog.sharetolearn.com/classroom-resources/growth-mindset-for-teachers/

- Dr. Dauma R. Touron. (June 1, 2016). *Memory Avoidance by Older Adults: When 'old dogs won't perform their 'new tricks'.* March 18, 2020. Available at https://www.ncbi.nlm.nih.gov/pmc/articles/PMC4465366/

- Alissa Rumsey. (March 28, 2017). *7 Ways to Perfect Your Morning Routine for Lasting Energy and Self-Control.* March 18, 2020. Available at https://health.usnews.com/health-news/blogs/eat-run/articles/2017-03-28/7-ways-to-perfect-your-morning-routine-for-lasting-energy-and-self-control

- Blackburn & Elrod. (2020). *How Smiling Affects You – And Those Around You!* March 18, 2020. Available at https://www.blackburnelrodortho.com/blog/how-smiling-affects-you-and-those-around-you

- Tuck/ (2019). *Productivity and Sleep.* March 18, 2020. Available at https://www.tuck.com/productivity-and-sleep/

- Christopher Friesen. (2016). *5 Learnable Mindsets of Highly Successful People.* March 18, 2020. Available at https://www.success.com/5-learnable-mindsets-of-highly-successful-people/

- Abbas, Raja, Darr, & Bouckenooghe. (2012). *Teacher's Turnover Intentions: Examining the Impact of Motivation and Organizational Commitment.* March 21, 2020. Available at https://www.researchgate.net/publication/308779545_Teacher's_Turnover_Intentions_Examining_the_Impact_of_Motivation_and_Organizational_Commitment

- Rick Snyder. (2002). *Hope Theory: Rainbows in the Mind.* 21, 2020. Available at: https://www.jstor.org/stable/1448867?seq=1

- Fred Luthans. (2011). *Organizational Behavior An Evidence-Based Approach 12 Edition.* March 21, 2020. Available at: https://bdpad.files.wordpress.com/2015/05/fred-luthans-organizational-behavior-_-an-evidence-based-approach-twelfth-edition-mcgraw-hill_irwin-2010.pdf

- Judge, T. and Watanabe, S. (1993). *Another Look at the Job Satisfaction-Life Satisfaction Relationship.* March 21, 2020. Available at https://psycnet.apa.org/record/1994-17491-001

- Lorenz, Beer, Pütz, & Heinitz. (2016). *Measuring Psychological Capital: Construction and Validation of the Compound PsyCap Scale (CPC-12)* March 21, 2020. Available at: https://journals.plos.org/plosone/article?id=10.1371/journal.pone.0152892

- Bandura, A. (1997). *Self-efficacy: The Exercise of Control.* March 21, 2020. Available at: https://psycnet.apa.org/record/1997-08589-000

1.1 Understanding habits

We develop common ways of thinking, hearing, speaking, moving, and perceiving. This includes all our signature behaviours, emotions, vocal habits, facial expressions, and mannerisms. Mental practices help us organize the experience, and our motor patterns make it possible to act quickly and automatically.

Consequently, a habit has positive value as a structure that allows us to cope with reality as it presents itself. It can have distinct drawbacks on the other hand. The propensity to rely on our usual ways of behaving and reacting can blind us to the novel and unusual, comfort us into seamlessness, prevent us from adapting to change, and deceive us into applying old solutions to new issues. Habits tend to work on an unconscious, automatic level. Generally, we don't know we're developing them, and we don't even realize we're using them. The golfer can rarely tell when he started to slice and may fail to recognise that as he swings, the ball spins. In every other sentence, the speaker who says, "as it was" has no idea that he does so until his wife points it out. In the psychology of perception, some of the most startling examples of unconscious action are found. The cues we use to see distance - perspective, colour, and variations in brightness - are so natural that we don't know we're using them.

How rigid are our perceptual habits? In response to this question, Stratton (1897) conducted a classic experiment in which he had subjects wear special lenses reversing the field of vision, both left and right and above and below. Surprisingly, it took the subjects only a few days to modify their deeply rooted habits, and they got used to be seeing down as up, and things that appeared on the right reached to the left.

Another experimenter, Foley (1940), not only distorted an adult monkey's visual field in these two ways but also made him see as far and as close as possible. The monkey reached, climbed, and walked practically within eight days. It took him three days to adjust when the lenses were removed revealing the standard perceptual field.

Willey et al. (1937) conducted a similar experiment with hearing using a device called a pseudo-phone. His human subjects wore earphones that transmitted sounds to the left ear from the right side, and vice versa. At first, this created confusion, but again the participants soon learned to adapt to the new conditions. These tests show that some of our most simple behaviours can be changed - a good thing to remember when you are called upon to adapt to new circumstances. The recruit may never like the food from the army, but he gets used to it, at least to some degree.

The person who uses a microscope for the first time is sure that he will not see anything more of a blur, but within a week or so, he begins to develop different viewing patterns that open up a new world of knowledge. The same thing occurs with the medical student as he slowly learns what to listen to when using a stethoscope.

The effect of early habit formation on the growth of the child's personality has been amply demonstrated by clinical research. Childhood disruptions can often be traced back to the time when the child acquired behavioural patterns associated with sleeping, weaning, speech, and elimination. It is now generally agreed that the parents' behaviour and the home environment are critical when teaching takes place. Encouragement, acceptance, and confidence not only promote the child's acquisition of good physical behaviours but also contribute to the development of healthy emotional patterns.

As pressure and reproof create anxiety or frustration, eventually they corrode relationships with oneself and others. Although both healthy and unhealthy habits tend to be permanent, it is crucial to recognize a curious persistence of neurotic tendencies. This is shown by the fact that when a person develops anxiety reactions in his adult life, he tends to go back to earlier habits that laid the foundation for this reaction. As a result, it set in a vicious cycle. Some of the latest behavioural therapies, such as the technique of J. Wolpe, (1990) are aimed at breaking these habits and creating new ones.

Some researchers view the process of learning in terms of habit-forming as it establishes a connection between a stimulus and a response that did not exist before. Verbal habits are a clear example: we learn to link to an instrument containing ink with the 'pen' response.

Theoretically, all other behaviours involving habit forming, such as the ability to ride a bicycle or the development of emotional reactions and attitudes, can also be viewed as learning appropriate responses to simple or complex stimuli.

Opponents of this view claim that learning is a mechanical process that lacks the role of cognitive processes. The 'cognitive' camp attempts to show that new, unexpected perspectives can be obtained from knowledge of concepts, while the 'habit' or 'associations' camp claims that all thinking and information can be clarified by either classical or operational conditioning from the single principle of creating stimulus-response ties.

Three other essential questions are raised by habit research.

- How many repetitions to implant a habit are necessary?
- Can a habit ever be completely lost once acquired?
- What's the best way of breaking a bad habit?

The first question does not have a single answer, but two significant developments have been made. Any repetition of an act appears to increase the strength of the habit somewhat, but the returns continue to decrease. This means we learn at the very beginning as fast as possible and should, therefore, be especially careful to start on the right foot. For example, in sports, it is advisable to get an expert's instruction so we can start forming the right habits at once. This prevents us from developing patterns that will have to be changed when it is incredibly difficult to do so.

Second, there is evidence that, without any repetition at all, certain behaviours can be formed based on single experiences. This appears to be the case where, as in traumatic experiences, emotions are involved. It may not extend to complex motor activities, although some parts may be established during the first trial, like the habit of placing one's foot on the clutch while driving a car. The topic of behaviour permanence has been explored for a long time.

Today, many psychologists believe that habits are never entirely lost, although more new or stronger habits can overlay them. There seems to be support for this hypothesis in the ease with which we revert to old motor behaviours like touch typing after many years — also in reviving old behaviour patterns in senile patients or individuals experiencing hypnotic regression (Ryder, 2014).

The problem can be answered, but not settled, at the moment of studying the memory process that potentially sheds some light on it.

Habit-breaking is another problem that cannot be solved with a single answer. The following are some of the most frequently discussed methods used by psychologists.

First, the incompatible-response:

Replacing the habit with a new antagonistic behaviour pattern. This approach is a way of 'counterconditioning' extinction— that is, by replacing it with a new one, it removes the initial response.

An example is a smoker who becomes accustomed to chewing when he feels like smoking. (Sometimes he ends up smoking and chewing at the same time!)

In applying this approach, as well as others, it is essential to follow the first two maxims suggested by William James in 1890: "We must be cautious about initiating an effort as deeply and determined as possible" and "Never suffer an exception until the new habit is firmly rooted in your life.

A boy caught smoking, for example, maybe forced to continue smoking until, essentially, he is ill. When this happens, the appetite for smoking will result in a new reaction, nausea, which will prevent the boy from continuing the habit.

For nail-biting, a similar technique can be applied. A form of fatigue is closely linked to 'deterrent treatments,' such as the use of Antabuse or hypnotic reinforcement in alcoholic addiction treatment.

Such approaches are types of behavioural therapy, like most habit-breaking strategies, and they do not seek to change the incentive that first created the pattern.

A method is toleration:

This is where a gradual introduction of stimuli raises an unwanted habit/reaction in small doses, so that more acceptable responses can be slowly established. For example, the child who fears grown dogs may react positively to a puppy, and this positive reaction will continue as he and the dog age; and eventually it will replace the fear. Likewise, through fun social experiences with one or two people, a shy person can sometimes overcome his timidity and gradually expand his acquaintances.

Kimble and Kendall (1953) found in animal studies that the method of toleration is superior to the method of exhaustion.

Another strategy is environmental change:

Getting away from the triggers or conditions that created a bad habit. This isn't always feasible— for starters, it's hard to get entirely away from smoking, and most people, just because they smoke, won't give up their old mates. Generally, a change of scene generates only temporary effects, although it may often work if the individual finds new satisfactions to replace those given by the original habit. This is counterconditioning again.

A good example is the approach of Alcoholics Anonymous. An essential part of the process is to find new leisure activities and new friends to make it unnecessary to seek other alcoholics' company or the bottle's companionship. Retribution is often used as a tool for breaking a habit, but it is probably the least successful of all methods. At best, it only briefly suppresses the undesirable habit, and usually only in the presence of the punisher. It does not encourage more favourable actions in itself and, instead, appears to be purely negative. However, it may perpetuate the bad habit; as a form of retaliation, the punished person may cling to it.

1.2 Difference between Habits and Addictions

In spite of unnecessary costs, addiction may be described as frequent involvement with anything due to a craving. This sounds like a habit, which also includes something done frequently. What are the dependency and behavioural variations and similarities?

Let's continue with some definitions of what looks like an addiction. After his first binge, a college freshman ends up in the emergency room but is not involved with alcohol again (although he may soon be). A pain control medical patient on opiates doesn't want the 'high' of the next injection but just seeks pain relief.

A low-stakes poker player has minor losses, but the gambling pleasure outweighs the cost to this individual. This last example shows that dependency depends heavily on the context in which it exists. It might not be as small a cost for one person as for another.

Now let's take the concept of addiction as an illness. The definition's 'three C's' are desire, effects, and (loss of) power. While commonly used, this definition's desire and control elements are inaccurate. The definition of the disease is all or none. You may or may not be an addict/alcoholic. There are several types of dependence, and in on all of them, you could be high, medium, or low. Where dependence starts is no clear dividing line. Second, it is understood that desire is uncontrollable. However, craving is entirely controllable with training. Otherwise, dependency is a state of hopelessness –but not!

Thankfully, everybody knows about the addictive behaviour's destructive consequences. The reason is that it's bad for you to switch an addictive behaviour! If you enjoy getting high, this increases the chances of harm to the body and mind, and eventually other areas of your life will also be negatively impacted.

We have a healthy addiction if the conduct in question produces more good than harm. A positive addiction is frequent involvement with a drug or behaviour, followed by a small amount of depression, with the benefits of participation outweighing the costs. The involvement of practice is compounded as costs and benefits are about the same. Interestingly, (harmful) addiction treatment requires successful addiction growth.

Seven hacks to change your habits in thirty days

Your life is controlled by what you focus on
- Tony Robbins

Chapter 2

This chapter provides a list of seven hacks by which you can easily change your bad habits and become the best you.

2.1 Realize the need to change

The first hack is to realize the need to change your bad habit. You understand that something is not right. This realisation happens when you get inspired by someone more successful or healthier than you. You want to be happy, healthy, and prosperous, like others. There are a few more factors that show signs that it's time to change your habits to fulfil your dreams.

2.2 Identify which habit to change

Now that you know that you need to change yourself to become a better person, the next step is to identify those habits that are harmful to you. The habit that creates difficulties for you in in the way of achieving your goals.

2.3 Replace the bad habit with a good habit

The third hack is to replace the identified habit with another that gives you same level of satisfaction; for example, if a person is trying to stop smoking, then he can chew gum if it gives him some pleasure. Then the bad habit can be replaced by gum; but if not, then you can try another habit and keep on trying different things until one gives you the same satisfaction.

2.4 Keep your willpower and motivation high

The purpose or why behind what you do is your motivation – in this case, it is behind the new habit you want. Motivation has different levels or layers with different strengths in each level or layer. Think of it as condensed circles. The circles like an onion in circles.

The outer layer is your big 'why' or motivating purpose.

Say you need to build some health and fitness habits: the big motivation of the outer layer is to be healthier and fitter as it makes you feel better, gives you more energy, gets you the most out of life, allows you to look better, all of which make you a happier person with stronger relationships.

Willpower is the power to put the will into action: to control what you are doing and to restrain yourself.

But the thing about will power is that you only have so much of it, and it's hard to rely on it when it runs out – because you are tired, hungry, or sad.

That's why you can wake up with a lot of willpower and good intentions, but it's harder to practice your will by evening.

2.5 Set goals

Setting goals is the process of choosing a target or objective you want to accomplish. Set smart goals that

- can be measured

- are attainable

- are appropriate

- are time-bound

2.6 Implementing plan measure your progress

Measurement is another secret to achieving long-term success of your goals. The human mind is fond of receiving feedback. Proof of our success is one of the most inspiring things we can encounter. That's why measurement is so critical to setting goals effectively. You gain insight into whether or not you are making progress by evaluating your performance.

A sample table of four weeks to change/track your habits

Days	M	T	W	T	F	S	S	Mark green if done	Mark red if not
Realization of change	If you are not happy with your life								
Identify bad habit	Eating too much	Stay away from temptations	Avoid going to restaurants frequently		Eat in portions				
Replace habit	Shift to good food	Try to eat grilled fish instead of fried	Eat baked potatoes instead of fries	Try oats instead of wheat	Try brown sugar instead of white	Take fresh juice instead of packed	Add lemon instead of fizzy drinks	Make green tea instead of a milkshake	
Motivation	Write it down and place it on your wall	Watch it in the morning to keep you motivated the whole day							
Goal	Weight loss	Measure your weight					Measure again		
Implementa-tion	Eat vegetables	Eat protein with veg	Eat more fruits	Eat brown rice			Veggie soup with chicken		
Meditation	For at least 5 min	Morning time is good for meditation	Go for a walk	If missed in the morning do it in the evening					

136

Hack 1- Realize the need to change

Everyone thinks of changing the world, but no one thinks of changing himself
- Leo Tolstoy

Chapter 3

Several factors force you to change yourself. When you are inspired by someone you try, or you wish you could be like, that person.

3.1 Inspiration

Anders Ericsson (1993) has been reminding us of the value of hard work for decades. The psychologist from the Florida State carried out a study that contributed to the so-called law of 10,000 hours. He and co-author Robert downplay the significance of native-born talent (even in people like Mozart) in their insightful new book, "Peak," in which is highlighted the importance of diligent practise - exhausting drills to refine your ability.

Anyone who has experienced excellence recognizes that Ericsson is fundamentally correct. The prerequisite for performance is hard effort. Yet there are times - after a lot of steady work and mastering the technical skills - when mind and spirit float. We call them inspiring moments.

Inspiration for what is a radical, countercultural, and spiritual movement is a much-used domesticated, amorphous, and secular term. Okay, bursts of inspiration according to normal logic don't make sense. They feel transcendent, irresistible, and uncontrollable. Time disappears or shifts its speed when one is motivated. The senses are strengthened. There may be goose bumps or shivering down the spine or feeling overwhelmed by beauty. Inspiration is always more important than pure admiration. There is an exciting feeling of acceleration, an energy blast, an understanding of expanded possibilities. The individual in the grip of inspiration has gained new insight and some holistic understanding, as if by chance, along with the feeling of being able to do more than what is expected.

Vladimir Nabokov believed in stages of inspiration. He wrote that there's the 'perfecting glow' and a 'tickly well-being' feeling that banishes all physical discomfort. The feeling is not yet giving up its identity, but a window has been opened, and some wind enters.

Then, after a few days, Nabokov continued that the writer 'feels what he's going to say.' There is a quick vision: the lightning bolt of inspiration that turns into a quick speech and a 'tumble of merging words' that forms the nucleus of a work that's going to grow from it over the months or years that follow.

An inspired job is different from normal life. First, as is usually understood, it's not about self-interest. A desire for money or promotion or prestige does not motivate it. The inspired person is driven by the work intrinsically. Such a person takes over the work.

Inspiration is not worth it. The time and effort invested prepare you for inspiration, but inspiration is a gift that goes beyond anything you might have deserved.

You can't control inspiration. Inspired people have lost some agency. They often feel that through them, something works, that some power is greater than themselves. The Greeks said there were the Muses. Believers may say it's either God or the Holy Spirit. Others might say it is a mysterious thing that bursts deep into the unconscious, as a new way of seeing.

Autonomous individuals don't get inspiration. It's a lovely contagion that goes through people. The word itself comes from the Latin, meaning "to breathe in." One inspiring achievement like the space program tends to elevate in others a sense of possibility; say, a little boy who dreams of being an astronomer. Then the inspired person performs his feats and inspires others, and so on. Inspiration is not solid and lasting. It's strong but short-lived; that's why so many people compare it to a wind. So people are waiting for his return when it's gone.

A Christian poet once wrote that inspiration is intrusive, transcendent, changing, yet also momentary and irregular. A poem can at once leave its author completely seized by nature and, in a deep way, separated from it; for as the act of making ends, the universe that seemed to overpower its limits becomes, once again, merely the world. It can be very difficult to retain confidence in that original moment of inspiration. That memory of that momentary blaze, and the art that emerged from it, can become a type of reproach to the fireless life in which you see yourself most of the time.

Most importantly, inspiration requires a certain posture, the kind that people feel when overwhelmed by something big and mysterious. They are both modest and self-assured, surrendering, and strong. We are willing to take a bold lark to something cool when inspired. We are bold enough to accept and try to express the craggy severity of reality in a new way.

Yes, to achieve this, hard work is really important. However, life is more mysterious than that.

3.2 Happenings that shows you need to change a habit

Life can be strangely complicated. You think you know what you desire; you've mapped it all out and your life probably isn't bad. However, you've settled, and your happiness fell by the wayside. These are key symptoms that you need a big life change. Whether you have been feeling like this for a few years or days, no one will lives their life just to go through the day. And let's be practical: You have more pressures and responsibilities, and you have to make major decisions. But it's tough. Running away and avoiding your life will not solve anything. Everything is usually determined by how you see the world and pick yourself up from a failure.

There is the notion that nothing is wrong with us, and we are filled with potential. We react to life situations, be they filled with trauma, stress, or dysfunctional relationships. Those who have faced/suffer at the hands of these life events the longest will not only grow more habitual to them, and build lower and lower expectations and dreams, but will also have less resiliency to handle change and stress. You have more energy and power than you give yourself credit for. However, if you're not exactly sure if your indifference has originated from your prevailing life condition or something else, there are symptoms that you need a significant life shift ASAP.

1. Your energy is low

When your strength is low from health issues, it's always best to visit the doctor. It could be as you're living a meaningless life, and you've just stopped caring. Maybe you have settled, and the idea of changing anything seems exhausting. You quit caring about yourself the way you once did. You require long walks, eating one healthy meal a day at least – trading off one junky snack for a healthy snack – and drink more water.

2. You feel paralyzed

Nothing inspires you anymore, and you don't recognize the last time you seriously laughed out loud. These little signs show you that you're not using your brains, so you can have a magnificent and interesting life. According to Mind Body Green, you might feel senseless because you have lost your passion and motivation. Try to do things that you like more often; it could help revitalize your soul.

3. You have stopped working on yourself

You are the most essential thing in your life, and it's crucial to remember to take care of yourself first because you won't be able to have a fulfilling life if you're not happy within. Go outside, research, start adopting 'me time,' and explore your world, be it through hobbies/activities with others. Try to find out and learn how vast your untapped abilities are. I can assure you that it will impress you.

4. Your environment is poisonous

If you find that you're with toxic people who always criticize you and your work, You are in a negative environment; it might be time to make some changes. It's difficult to be positive when your surroundings are not giving you happiness.

Your friends do not pump you up; rather, they enjoy listening to your down moments and require you to hear theirs regularly. In fact, they may celebrate your distress. They try to put you down in small ways that just don't feel right, but you may not be able to pinpoint situation - maybe it is the back-handed praise or someone cutting in when you are talking; maybe it is never showing up on time, not having remorse after a tiff, or treating you as a side person. In any case, such people waste your energy, resources, and tolerance.

5. You're not happy in your romantic relationship

Sometimes it's hard to admit that the one you are with isn't your romantic partner. Whether they are poisonous and bring you down, or your life goes on separate paths, it may be a good idea to stop fighting and just pull the plug. Your partner makes you feel less than you are in some way. They blame and use you as their emotional punching bag; and if it's physical abuse, then you need leave right now.

6. You're merely surviving

Losing yourself will ruin your imagination and motivation by doing the same mundane things. Going home from work and just paying the bills can be detrimental to the spirit. Your life should be packed with opportunities and challenges. Daydreaming about something you want without action is not going to get you far in life. If you felt anxious and excited, your gut might be telling you that you need a quick adjustment.

7. You have adopted a compulsive behaviour

You can't stop eating, smoking, or drinking. Compulsive behaviour is a sign that we're struggling to balance the voice of reason with the desires of your hearts. Addiction becomes a friend with whom you both celebrate and condone. Hold your vices apart and figure out the problem's origin so that you can fix it and live the life you have always wanted to live.

8. You're always dreaming of the past

Although remembering stuff is always good, you don't want to focus solely on the past because you're sick of your present-day life. According to the Huffington Post, Annabel Irion, a one hundred-year-old psychology and marketing professor at the University of Texas, an Art Marksman and Ph.D., if you look back on past events, you know how they worked out. Uncertainty is overwhelming. The present sometimes feels less fun than the past, because we're still waiting to find out how the different educational and business projects are going.

You keep on thinking that there has to be more than this. It may be time to change things around if you don't feel like its meaningful to your life. You may be looking for it or waiting patiently for signs for what it could be; but ultimately, if you are constantly waiting for the answers to come to you, you may never live your fullest life. Many people tend to wait for permission to live the life they've always dreamed of, according to the spiritual site Tiny Buddha, but no one else will give them access besides them.

9. While your life won't be filled with sunshine and butterflies

Every time you wake up, it shouldn't make you feel sad. Depression is your body and brain's way of saying that something has to change. It's there as a signal to make you stop and think again and hopefully do something else. You can start taking better care of yourself, saying 'no' to things or individuals that aren't healthy for you, seeking others' help, or changing your life situation. Whatever it is, it's one way to know it's time to change.

10. If your physical/mental health is deteriorating badly

It's time for a big change in your life. If there's one thing that's a sure sign of a need for improvement, it's stress. If you're living under immense stress at work, home, or in your social life, it's time to make a change. Change your habits like sleeping, dieting, and exercise. Be aware of how you interact with your body. Feeling worn out and drained is a crucial indication that, in some way, your life needs to be changed.

You will need to decide how you want to live your life, since no one else will. Pick yourself up, find out what you want, and go after it instead of feeling helpless and defeated. Don't forget to respect yourself, and don't settle. You deserve more than that.

3.3 Changing everyday habits will have an impact

Adapting to change: why it matters in our lives

The rule of life is change. Those that look only to the past or the present will surely miss the future, said John F Kennedy. We can't avoid it, and the tougher life gets, the more we resist change. Improvement according to Kennedy is a life policy. Transition surrounds us. It is the one thing that affects our lives the most drastically. As it will find you, there is no escaping transition. It will push you and pressure you to rethink how to live your life.

We're going to look at the significance of change and how you can adapt to an ever-changing life. Why do you have to change?

By chance, life doesn't get better; it gets better through change, says Jim Rohn. Change can come into our lives as a result of a crisis, a choice or just by chance. We're all faced with having to choose: will we make the change or not?

It's better to be ready for change as we have more influence over how we react to the changes we face in our lives. You have little control or options as to how you want to live your life when you are poorly prepared and slow to change. You are living your life as a conservative rather than a change activator.

Life is a series of spontaneous and natural changes. Do not fight them; it just causes sorrow. Let's make our reality. Let things flow naturally in whatever way we like says Lao Tzu. We can't avoid the unforeseen events (crises) in our lives, which are the events that challenge and force us to leave our comfort zone. When we neglect or hide from the challenge of change, the ability to learn and grow is denied to us.

To survive is to evolve; to change is to mature; to mature is to go on making oneself endlessly—Henri Bergson. Our resilience in life can only grow stronger if we accept change and handle difficulties in a positive way instead of hiding and neglecting the possibilities that change can bring.

The effect that change can bring into one's life is no escape. Managing life change is essential to living a life in which you not only survive but also succeed.

3.4 Adapting to Change Strategies

The five strategies below are key steps that will allow you to adapt and manage change successfully in your life.

1. Changing Your Mindset – Your Power Option

Change is impossible without improvement, and those who are unable to change their minds cannot change anything says George Bernard Shaw. We are living our lives in our comfort zone. This is what our unconscious wants because it is the "known." Embracing change enters the unknown, and our subconscious doesn't like the "unknown," so it's going to resist it.

145

As we confront the destructive effects of transition, our anxiety and self-limiting values will kick into motion. The fact that change is a disruptor does not escape us, and it feels uncomfortable and frightening. However, it is a choice that allows us to bring about positive change.

We can't control the changing events in our lives, but we can control how we respond to the impact these events have on.

Life is a matter of choice. Some of us are sorry; some of us are proud. Some are going to haunt us forever. The message is: we are what we have decided to be (Graham). The more you use your decision power, and the more you concentrate your attitude on adapting to change positively, the more prepared you are to cope with the effect that change will bring to your life.

2. Find meaning in life: get out of your zone of comfort

Comfort zones are the enemies of achievement, where unrealized dreams are buried. 'Leadership starts when you step outside your comfort zone' -Roy T. Bennett. Knowing what's important gives you purpose and knowledge of how you want to live your life. You have insight and concentration with a sense of purpose and meaning, and these two elements are vital to be able to successfully adjust and handle the effect of change in life.

Having no purpose or meaning means that within the boundaries of your comfort zone, you continue to drift. The purpose and meaning of life give you the courage to leave your comfort zone, where you will experience change and the possibilities it can bring.

3. Let go of regrets

'The fact is, unless you let go, unless you forgive yourself, unless you forgive the circumstance, unless you know the situation is over, you can't move forward.' – Steve Maraboli. Regrets have a tremendous impact on how you respond to change, and they hold you back in life. It is significant to be able to move forward and let go of regrets.

It is the events of transition that create opportunities in life, so you may miss the possibilities of the present and the future if you look only to your past. You can't change what you have or haven't done, so let it go. The only power that you now have is choosing to live in a present and future life.

Blowing up a bunch of balloons and writing a regret on each is a great exercise to deal with disappointments in life. Then, let go of the balloons. As the balloons float away, say goodbye to regrets clearly.

This is a straightforward but effective way to deal with the pile of regrets you have gathered in your life.

4. Write a list of scary things to do–then go do them

Change is scary, and it's all about stepping into the unknown and out of your comfort zone. The unconscious wants to get out of our comfort zone and do frightening things. In reality, we want to train our subconscious to think that it is a normal thing to step out of our comfort zone and do scary things.

Make a list of scary things you'd like to do but were too afraid of. Put a plan in motion and do it afterwards. Go have fun, challenge yourself, and take advantage of the feeling of being frightened and entering the unknown.

Public speaking to me and many other individuals is one of the most terrifying things to do. The first speech was a nightmare to overcome my problem with public speaking. My knees were knocking (didn't know it was possible, but it is!), and when I started, I broke out in a sweat and my voice was a whisper.

I got through it, and although it wasn't the most celebrated speech, it was amazing to overcome my fear. I kept going and knew that I enjoyed talking so much to the public that I jumped at any chance to speak thereafter.

5. Maintaining the body in good health

'To keep the body in good health is a duty. Otherwise, you won't be able to keep your mind sharp and clear.' –Buddha

Living a balanced and active life builds resilience and the ability to successfully manage the disruption that change can have in your lives.

Stress is a normal response to everyday life changes and challenges. Stress can help you work better under pressure short term, but constant stress can present health problems. Finding positive ways to cope with the stress and pressure we face daily is key to physical and emotional survival.

Hack 2- Identify your bad habit

A habit cannot be tossed out of the window; it must be coaxed down the stairs a step at a time
- Mark Twain

Chapter 4

Habits are the way the brain supports us by creating a pattern that neurons will obey. They put us on autopilot. They may be the slaves or masters of your life. Through promoting bad patterns, most people choose the latter. Instead of doing their job, they waste time before their smartphones or staring at TV screens.

Between presentations, they stress out because they cannot shake their procrastination.

We are struggling with weight and health because bad eating habits cannot be reversed. When we change, we feel good, but afterwards, we feel bad. We promise to break the bad habit, but are unable to resist temptation. We promise to do it until the idea disappears into tomorrow.

When you have bad habits, there's nothing to be sorry about: everybody's got bad habits. Being open to breaking them gives you an advantage over most people who deny them.

If you can't accept that something has to change, you can't change something.

Small, bad behaviours can have a negative long-term effect when piled up. In terms of productivity, your bad habits may create a dent.

Most are unable to acknowledge that the findings obtained today are the sum of what is repeatedly done. No wonder the power of habits only benefits a few.

4.1 The Power of Habits in our Lives

A young woman is walking into a lab. She has changed almost every part of her life over the past two years. She quit smoking, ran a marathon, and was promoted at work. Neurologists discovered that the patterns within her brain have fundamentally changed.

Procter & Gamble's marketers are studying videos of people who make their beds. They desperately try to sell a new product called Febreze, on its way to becoming the biggest flop in the history of the company. Immediately, one of the marketers notices an almost imperceptible pattern and Febreze manages to earn a billion dollars a year with a slight shift in ads.

An untested CEO takes over one of America's largest companies. His first business order attacks a single pattern among his employees - how they approach worker safety - and soon the company, Alcoa, becomes a Dow Jones top performer.

What's in common with all these people? By focusing on patterns that shape every area of our lives, they have achieved success. They succeeded in changing habits.

The award-winning business reporter for the New York Times, Charles Duhigg, takes us to the exciting edge of scientific discoveries that explain why there are habits and how they can be changed. Duhigg brings to life a full new understanding of human nature and its potential for transformation with penetrating intelligence and the ability to distil vast amounts of information into absorbing narratives.

Along the way, researchers learn why, despite years of trying, some people and companies are struggling to change, while others appear to be remaking themselves overnight. We visit laboratories where neuroscientists are investigating how habits work and exactly where they reside in our brains. We find out how the right habits have been crucial to the success of Michael Phelps, the Olympic swimmer, Howard Schultz, the Starbucks CEO, and Martin Luther King, Jr., the civil rights hero. They go inside Procter & Gamble, Target Superstores, Saddleback Church of Rick Warren, NFL locker rooms, and the nation's largest hospitals and see how the adoption of so-called keystone behaviours can mean billions and the difference between failure and success, life and death.

The power of habit has a compelling case at its core: it's the secret to regular exercise, weight loss, raising excellent children, becoming more successful, creating innovative businesses and social movements, and achieving success. It's recognizing how habits work

Habits aren't fate. As Charles Duhigg shows, we can reshape our businesses, our communities, and our lives by harnessing this new science.

4.2 How Good Habits and Bad Habits are Formed

Habits are omnipresent, and we probably all think we know what a habit is. Wendy Wood is entirely right. More than 80% of people say they understand habits in conducted surveys. But when you change your actions, how effective are you? Can you make changes and stick to them? These same people say, 'Hmm, no, not very often.' Thus, they are not affected by what other people understand.

Habits are a tool for training. All we need to do is repeat something and get praised for it to develop a habit. In research, it has been found that in the same context, about 43% of what people do every day is repeated, usually while thinking about something else. They react automatically without making any real decisions. And that's the pattern. A habit is a kind of cognitive shortcut for doing what we have done in the past that has worked for us and given us some satisfaction.

Most of you think that self-control can force you to do things you don't want to do. Some people have super-will and others don't. Many people confuse their habits and self-control. In surveys, most say you have to exercise restraint to start a new habit, and that's just not true. The problem with self-control is that we all know people who are not effective in almost every area of their lives, and psychologists have built metrics to classify these individuals by assessing how much self-control they have.

The people on the survey scales that rank high tend to weigh less than the rest of us. They're more likely to have saved enough retirement money. They have happier relationships, and at work they're more productive, while at school, they get better grades. These things are connected to what we consider to be self-control. Yet recent research by Angela Duckworth and her colleagues has shown a curious contradiction: by exercising control, people who score high are not achieving success in life. By white knuckling through life, they don't practice self-denial. They know how to create patterns that meet their goals.

We consider that about 43% of what people do every day to be replicated, typically in the same way as if they're afraid of something. People who have high self-control instead are very good at developing the right behaviours to achieve excellent results in life. We seem to grasp the power of circumstances and choose those in which the desired behaviour are easiest to replicate. Such people don't have a lot of 'friction' in their lives, so they're not inclined to act counterproductively.

It feels that changing our self-control perspective can help us reclaim our sense of self-worth and become more childish. Instead of constantly berating ourselves – 'Oh man, I've done this thing again that I didn't want to do' - we should change our environment.

That's self-control's flip side. It's great to say, 'Yeah, I have a lot of self-control, and I'm excellent at resisting temptation,' but we fail so often and then feel like failures. It frees us from a very negative kind of life.

At M&M research teaches us how some of our health goals could potentially be undermined? It was a study of carrots and M&Ms (Pei-Ying Lin, 2015), In a computer game, people were asked to select carrots. When they were hungry and everyone played this game, and they got the carrots. Once they saw them on the screen, they had to push a joystick in the direction of the carrots, and then they won carrots and had to eat them. They all liked broccoli, but they also enjoyed cookies. And after they trained people to pick carrots by moving the joystick to the carrots whenever they saw them on the screen, they gave them the chance to pick M&M's if they wanted to. Now, people continued to select carrots when the screen was set up in the same way as during training. The carrots were chosen by more than 60%. But when the screen changed and the joystick had to be moved in a different direction, they stopped thinking and many went for M&M's.

It was found that people fall back on good as well as bad habits when they are distracted or feel unusually tired or overwhelmed.

This turns upside down the conventional thinking about habits. People think that patterns are bad things when they don't care about what they want. Yet they developed beneficial habits in the study to choose healthy food when they thought about it.

We generally think of top-down executive control as our 'good self.' But can pausing to think be the thing that prevents us from taking sustainable transportation or going to the gym if we had first set up those habits?

In many other studies, it was found that when people are affected or feel unusually tired or overwhelmed, they rely on good as well as bad habits. Their power over the executive is kind of off grid. They're worried about things going on in their lives or are too tired to make real decisions. We see both a boost in the performance of both good and bad habits. It is shocking because we like to believe that our self-conscious, executive regulation is well-intentioned and will help us achieve our goals.

Example of a woman

There are three sisters, and they all have young children. Their nieces and nephews were between two months and seven years of age. Young children can interfere with routine and lead to fewer repetitive behaviours for parents who, despite having young children, are trying to create good new habits.

One of the fascinating things that arose early in this study was that if one lives with other people, especially children, you have fewer overall behaviours than others simply because of the delays caused by the people in your life. An important thing was found when a mother with young children found a time and place to enjoy some control. It was 6:00 a.m. for her, as the children usually slept until 7:00 a.m. She used it for an hour of exercise and would go home in time to serve breakfast and send the kids off to class. At other times of the day, she tried to set up good exercise habits, and it just didn't work because the children always had to go to the doctor or to a friend's house or to practice or play sports. Unlike early in the morning, she didn't have much control over the rest of the day. So you must find the most consistent time of the day that is uninterruptedly yours and focus on building your habits there.

What tends to make it so difficult is the unforeseen situation of doing things automatically. We still make habits. For example, as part of their relationship, a husband and wife have many shared habits. They eat breakfast and dinner together. They have interconnected patterns, and these patterns are as important as the trends in the rest of our world. We debate the patterns we're trying to form with other people. And if we've been in a relationship that has ended, it's incredible how much our behaviour changes as that other person is no longer cueing the appropriate response. You miss the cue of your habit. It may not be a very romantic way of thinking about relationships, but it is a specific way of thinking.

Example of a girl

As a girl moved to a new city to start graduate school a year ago, she picked up a habit she always wanted: cycling as a primary form of transportation. Why is a transition or another big change in life, like the end of a relationship, a time to pick up good habits and break bad ones?

We find these changes in life to be very challenging, unwanted, and difficult; but they are opportunities as well. That thinking can get in the way, but it can also be an opportunity to begin to align our habits with our values.

Starting with restructuring your life takes some time, but when you no longer have those signals from your old background, you're freed up. Making new choices is like a window of opportunity.

Many of us may also have had the opposite experience of living in one place and developing a habit, but then we move and lose that routine and habit that had taken months or years to build. How resilient is changing habits, and is it essential to practice the new pattern for a long time? Well, time contributes to the strength of the habit, so the longer you've done something, the stronger the habits will be.

Research on transferring students to a new university has been done. What was found is that if the context at the new school is similar to the old one for those with strong habits, then they maintained their habits. People continue to exercise just as they did at their old university if they had a gym in both places; for example, in their apartment. They could just pick up the habit and go on. But if they moved to a new apartment without a gym, and there wasn't one nearby, or if there was only one running track and weights were usually lifted, they lost their habit.

One of the most important messages that all of us rely on is the context in which we live. Behaviours are usually based on what's comfortable and satisfying, i.e., what's easy for us to do over and over again and what's rewarding, It comes from our backgrounds and the places we live in. People across the country are witnessing different types of conditions in different states. We see people in the U.S. with different habits. People in Colorado, D.C., and Alaska, for example, exercise more than many other parts of the country, and they tend to be healthier as well. Some of this is that healthy people choose to go to those locations, but some of it is also that places affect us once we get there, prompting a better, more active lifestyle. And this has implications for our health and well-being.

All of us shape behaviours based on what's easy to do over and over again. The best proof we have is that forming a simple habit can take two to three months to make something so automated that you don't have to think about it.

A query is how often do I have to repeat something to make it a habit; and conventional wisdom is 21 days, but that's just not true. It's like when you begin to tie your shoes. You put on and tie your shoes, and you don't even have to will it. Instead, it seems to flow when you think of something else.

So, be patient and in it for the long haul, and don't give up.

Hack 3- Replace the bad habit

It is easier to prevent bad habits than break them
- Benjamin Franklin

Chapter 5

The mind, like the body, embraces any habit you want to touch by practice --Socrates.

Habits are hard to alter because they are embedded within us. To make the action automatic, do things regularly to condition your neurons. That's why when you do your morning routine, your brain does not make a conscious effort. Bad habits are obstacles that divert you from your goals. They slow your progress.

A lot of people want to stop them. They are unable to improve despite their best efforts. They're taking their patterns to a place they don't want to.

Bad habits, as they make a person feel good, are hard to break. Dr. Russell Poldrack said that the patterns of pleasure are more challenging to break. When it experiences enjoyable behaviour, the brain releases the chemical dopamine. He said, if you do anything again and again and when you do it, the dopamine is there, and it makes the habit much deeper. Dopamine induces the urge to do it again when you don't do those things. 'People have different behaviours, so the way they break them is different from person to person'.

To nail what works for you, it takes a lot of trial-and-error. No one-size-fits-all formula can be followed by everyone.

Some science-based ways to help break or mitigate your bad habits:

5.1 Ways to Bid Your Bad Habits Goodbye

Identify your habit loop
While devouring a pack of chips or procrastinating, you have one bad habit you want to bid goodbye. When habits get formed, our brains

work hard when we first participate in a new task- processing tons of new data as we find our way. But the behaviour begins to become automatic as soon as we understand how a task works, and the mental activity needed to do the job decreases dramatically.

Think about how much brainpower and focus you had to use when you first parked a car, or even when you tied your shoelaces for the first time. Equate that with the amount of mental effort you are making now.

Charles Duhigg (2014) writes, 'This process - in which the brain transforms a series of behaviours into an unconscious routine - is known as "chunking", and it's at the heart of how habits develop. There are thousands, if not hundreds, of behavioural chunks that we depend on every day.'

How Habit Loops Work

Habits consists of a simple, but compelling, three-step cycle. Per Duhigg, first, there's a cue, or a signal that tells the brain to go into automatic mode and use it. Then there is the routine that can be psychological or physical or mental. Finally, there's a bonus to help the brain find out if it's worth remembering this particular loop for the future. This chain becomes more and more automatic over time. The warning and reward are intertwined until a strong sense of anticipation and desire arises.

The first principle of habit-changing is that you have to play by the rules. That is, the three-step process (e.g., cue, routine, reward) doesn't escape since it is hard-wired into our minds. If you wish to get rid of a bad habit, you need to figure out how to execute a better routine and deliver the same reward. Let's presume that at the end of a long day you like to go out with your friends and have a few drinks. There are generally two benefits in this situation:

(1) The eventual socialization that happens and

(2) The alcohol's calming effects on your nervous system

These two incentives are both valid and appropriate. You'll still be miserable if you delete alcohol from your life but replace it with nothing else. The key is to keep the cue and the incentives (e.g., social time, relaxation) when adjusting the routine (e.g., drinking).

An alternative approach might be to convince a co-worker or friend after work to start exercising with you - running, yoga, rock climbing, or anything that works. You then have a balanced routine (exercise) replacing the unhealthy habit (drinking) while offering the same benefits.

If you wish to get rid of a bad habit, it is necessary to figure out how to implement a healthier routine to get the same reward.

How Habits Work

The hard thing about studying habit science is that most people want to know the secret formula to change a habit quickly when they hear about this field of research. When scientists discover how these patterns work, then it is fair that they also need to find a quick-change formula, right? If it were just that easy.

It's not that there are no equations; the challenge is that to change habits, there is not one equation. There are thousands.

Individuals and behaviours are all different, so the nuances of diagnosing and modifying patterns in our lives vary from individual to individual and behaviour to behaviour. Giving up smoking is different from curbing over-consumption, which is different from adjusting how you interact with your partner, which is different from how you perform work tasks. What's more, different cravings drive the habits of each person.

As a consequence, there is no one prescription offered in this book. Instead, I was hoping to offer something else: a structure for understanding how patterns work and a guide for playing with how they might change. Some behaviours make evaluating and influencing simple. Others are more complex and stubborn, requiring lengthy study. And for others, the transition is never a complete operation.

But that doesn't mean that it can't happen. It might not be quick to change, and it's not always easy. But with time and effort, it is possible to reshape almost any habit.

The framework:

- Identify the daily habit
- Take the incentive test
- Isolate the cue
- Have a strategy

Step one: identify the routine

Researchers found a simple neurological pathway at the heart of every habit, a loop consisting of three parts:

- a cue
- a routine and
- a reward

You have to identify the components of your loops to understand your habits. You can look for ways to replace old vices with new routines once you have diagnosed the habit loop of a particular behaviour.

As an example, say you have a problematic habit of going to the cafeteria and buying a chocolate chip cookie every afternoon. You've gained a few pounds from this habit - exactly 8 pounds - and your wife has made a couple of pointed remarks. You've also gone so far as to put a post-it on your screen that reads NO MORE COOKIES.

Yet you manage to ignore the note every afternoon, get up, walk to the cafeteria, buy a cookie, and eat it while sitting around the cash register with colleagues. It feels good, and it feels terrible afterwards. You promise yourself that tomorrow you will collect the courage to resist. It's going to be different tomorrow. But the habit retakes hold tomorrow.

How do you diagnose this behaviour and then change it? Through working out the pattern of the habit, and defining the routine is the first step. As with most behaviours, the most apparent thing in this cookie scenario is the attitude you want to alter. Your routine is to get up in the afternoon from your office, walk to the cafeteria, buy and eat a chocolate chip cookie while chatting with friends. So that's what you put in the loop. Next, a few less obvious questions are what's this routine's cue? Is that hungry? Are you bored? Low on energy? When you dive into another task, you need a break? And what is the payment? The cookie alone? The scene change? The threat of the temporary? Will you socialize with your colleagues? Or is it the power burst that comes from that sugar blast?

You should do a little research to work this out.

Step two: experiment with rewards

Rewards are efficient in their fulfilment of cravings. Yet, we are often unaware of the cravings that motivate our behaviours. When the marketing team from Febreze realized, for instance, that customers wanted a fresh smell at the end of a cleaning routine, they found a desire that nobody knew existed. In plain sight, it was hidden. Most cravings are like this: retrospectively obvious, but incredibly challenging to see when we're under their sway.

It is useful to experiment with different incentives and find out which cravings influence specific behaviours. It can take a couple of days, or a week or longer. You shouldn't feel any pressure during this time to make a real change; think of yourself in the data collection stage as a scientist.

If you feel the urge to go to the cafeteria to buy a cookie on the first day of your experiment, change your routine to provide a different incentive. For example, go for a walk outside, perhaps around the block, instead of going to the cafeteria and just return to your desk without eating anything. Go to the cafeteria the next day and buy a doughnut or a candy bar at your desk and eat it. Go to the cafeteria the next day, buy an apple and eat it as you talk with your family. Then, try a cup of coffee. Instead of going to the cafeteria, go for a few minutes to a friend's office to chat and go back to your desk.

You get the idea. What you choose to do is not as important as not buying a cookie. The aim is to test various theories to decide what causes the craving. Do you want the cookie itself, or do you want a break from work? If it's the cookie, are you hungry? (In which case an apple would work as well.) Or is it because you want the cookie's power burst? (So coffee should be enough.) Or, are you walking up the cafeteria as an excuse for socializing, and the cookie is just a convenient excuse? (If so, it should satisfy the temptation to walk to someone's office and talk for a few minutes.)

You may use an old trick to look for patterns when you test four or five different rewards: after each activity, jot down the first three things that come to mind when you get back to your desk on a piece of paper. These may be feelings, random thoughts, observations on how you feel, or just the first three words that come into your head. Then set the alarm for 15 minutes on your watch or phone. Tell yourself when time is up: do you still feel the urge for this cookie?

The explanation of why writing down three things is necessary is as follows. Even though they are meaningless words, they induces a momentary perception of what you think or feel. A note card loaded with comments can be a push into the consciousness of our desires, so writing three words will force a moment of focus. However, studies also show that writing down a few words helps us recall what we thought at the time. When we review our notes at the end of the experiment, remembering what we thought and felt at that precise moment will be much easier because our scribbled words will trigger a wave of memory.

And why the warning of 15 minutes? Because these tests aim to decide the desired reward. If you still have a desire to get up and go to the cafeteria fifteen minutes after eating a doughnut, then your addiction is not driven by a craving for sugar. If you still want a cookie after chattering at a colleague's desk, then the need for human contact is not what is driving your behaviour.

On the other hand, if you find it easy to get back to work fifteen minutes after talking with a friend, then you have recognized in the incentive a temporary relaxation and socialization that your addiction tried to fulfil.

You can isolate what you crave by experimenting with different rewards, which is essential in redesigning the habit. Once the routine and the reward have been worked out, what remains is to identify the cue.

Step three: isolate the cue

Approximately ten years ago, a psychologist at the University of Western Ontario tried to answer a problem that had puzzled social scientists for years: Why do some eyewitnesses misremember what they see, while others correctly recall events?

The eyewitnesses' memories are incredibly important, of course. And yet studies show that eyewitnesses sometimes misremember what they were doing. For example, when wearing a skirt, a woman may insist that the robber was a man or the crime occurred at dusk, while police reports say it happened at 2:00 in the afternoon. On the other hand, eyewitnesses will recall incidents witnessed with a near-perfect memory.

This phenomenon has been investigated by dozens of studies, trying to determine why some people are better eyewitnesses than others. Studies have theorized that some people simply have better memories, or that it is easier to remember a crime that happens in a familiar place. But those hypotheses were not checked; people with strong and weak memories, who are more and less familiar with a crime scene, are equally likely to misremember what happened.

A University of Western Ontario psychologist has taken a different approach. She wondered if researchers made a mistake by concentrating on what had been said by questioners and witnesses, rather than how they said it. She thought the interviewing process is affected by implicit signals. But she couldn't see anything as she watched videotape after videotape of witness interviews, looking for these signals. There was so much movement in each interview that she could not discern any trends: not the facial expressions, the ways the questions were asked, nor the fluctuating emotions.

So she came up with an idea: she drew up a list of a few things that she would concentrate o: the voices of the questioners, the witnesses' facial expressions, and how close the witnesses and questioners stood together. She then eliminated all details from those things that would confuse her. She turned up the volume on the television, so all she could sense was the sound of the questioners' voices instead of hearing words. She taped a paper over the faces of the questioners, so the expressions of the witnesses were all she could see. To measure their distance from each other, she put a tape measure on the monitor.

And once she began studying particular items, patterns kept jumping out. She saw that cops who used a soft, friendly tone were generally confronted by witnesses who misremembered evidence. Witnesses who smiled more or stood closer to the person asking the questions were more likely to misremember.

In other words, witnesses were more likely to misremember what had happened when environmental signs said 'we are friends'– as in a friendly voice or smiling face. Maybe it was because these signs of friendship subconsciously triggered a habit of pleasing the questioner.

The significance of this experiment is that dozens of other researchers had watched the same tapes. Many smart people had seen the same trends, but no one had understood them because each tape contained too much information to see a subtle cue.

But, once the psychologist decided to focus on only three behaviour categories and remove the alien data, the patterns leapt out. This is the same way we live our lives. The reason why it is so difficult to identify the indications that trigger our habits is that as our behaviours unfold while too much information is bombarding us. Tell yourself, do you eat breakfast every day because you're hungry at a particular time? Or because it says 7:30 on the clock? Or when did your kids start to eat? Maybe because you're dressed, that's when the habit of breakfast kicks in?

What causes the action when you turn your car left while driving to work? A sign on the street? A specific tree? In reality, it is the awareness that this is the right route. Are they all together? If you drive your kid to school, and you find that you've been absentmindedly on the path to work and not to school, what caused the mistake? What was the thought that made you 'drive to work', instead of the pattern of 'drive to school?'

We can use the same method as the therapist to locate a signal in the middle of the noise: defining groups of activities scrutinized to see trends. Luckily, in this respect, science provides some support. Experiments have shown that almost all the usual indications fit these categories:

- location
- time
- emotional state
- other people
- immediate preceding action

If you are trying to find out the cue for the habit of going to the cafeteria and buying a chocolate chip cookie, you should write down five things when the urge hits. These are my actual notes when I was trying to diagnose my habit.

- What time is it? (3:36 pm)
- What are you doing (sitting at my desk)?
- What is your state of emotion? (bored)
- Who else was there? (none)
- What was the previous action before the urge? (replied to an email)

The next day:

- Where are you? (returning the copier)
- What time is that? (3:18) and what is your state of emotion? (happy)
- Who else is there? (Jim from Sports)
- What was the previous action? (made a photocopy)

Day 3:

- Where are you? (meeting room)
- What time is that? (3:41 pm)
- What is your state of emotion? (I'm sick of the plan I'm working on)
- Who else is there? (editors come to the meeting)
- What was the previous operation before the urge? (I sat down because the meeting was about to begin)

It was pretty clear three days ago what cue activated my cookie addiction. I felt the need to get a snack at a particular time. I had already learned in step two that my conduct was not motivated by hunger. The bonus I was hoping for was a temporary distraction, the kind that comes from a friend's gossip. And the habit was activated between 3:00 and 4:00.

Step four: have a plan

Once you've worked out the habit cycle, you've established the incentive that activates your conduct, the stimulus that causes it, and the pattern itself so you can start to change your behaviour. By preparing for the cue and selecting an action that provides the reward you want, you will switch to a better routine. It's a plan that you need.

We learned in the prologue that a habit is a choice we make deliberately at some point and then stop thinking about it, but keep doing it, often every day.

To put it another way, a habit is a rule that our brain automatically follows: I will do a ROUTINE to get a REWARD when I see CUE (Charles Duhigg, 2014).

We need to start making decisions again to re-engineer the equation. And, according to study after study, the easiest way to do this is to have a strategy. Such preparations are known as 'implementation goals' within the field of psychology. Take, for example, my afternoon cookie addiction. By using this method, I discovered that in the afternoon, my cue was at about 3:30. I knew my routine was going to the cafeteria, buying a cookie, and chatting with friends. And, through experimenting, I discovered it wasn't the cookie I wanted: it was a moment of fun and a chance to socialize.

So, I wrote a plan: I'm going to go to a friend's office every day at 3:30 and chat for 10 minutes. I fixed the alarm on my watch for 2:30 to make sure I remembered. It wasn't working right away. I was busy for a few days, ignored the warning, and then fell off the wall. Sometimes, having a friend willing to talk seemed like too much hassle: it was easier to get a cookie, so I gave up on the desire. But on the day that I followed my plan - when my alarm went off - I forced myself to walk to a friend's office and talk for 10 minutes. I found that I was feeling better at the end of the working day. I didn't go to the kitchen and didn't eat a cookie, so I felt pretty good. Finally, it got automatic: I found a friend when the alarm rang and ended the day feeling a real sense of achievement. I didn't think about the routine after a couple of weeks. Then I went to the cafeteria, bought tea and drank it with friends when I couldn't find anyone to talk to.

That was all-around six months ago. I no longer have to look at my watch at some point. But I'm absentmindedly standing up at around 3:30 every day, searching the newsroom for someone to talk to, wasting 10 minutes chattering about the news, and then returning to my office. It's happening almost without knowing about it. It has become a custom.

5.2 It's not that "I can't," But "I Don't."

Houston University researchers conducted an experiment in which one group was instructed to use 'I can't,' while the other used 'I don't.' A granola bar or some chocolate was given after the test. 39% of people who used 'I can't' selected the granola bar, while it was preferred by 64% of people who used 'I don't' instead of chocolate.

This experiment shows the importance of choosing a word and how it can affect a person's motivation. Rather than thinking, 'I can't eat potato chips,' reframe it as 'I don't eat potato chips.' It's kind of telling yourself you're not doing the behaviour.

If they answer with 'I can't', most people are easily convinced by others.

Are you acquainted with it?

'Check this here. Only one glass of beer.' 'No, that's not something I should drink.' 'Oh, don't be a child. You will not be destroyed by one shot.' 'I can't. I can't do that. Yeah, just one.' Unlike: 'I'm not drinking beer. My body's not reacting well.'

5.3 Replacing the Bad Habit with a Good Habit

It can be hard to stop something. Psychologist Timothy Pitchy (Maltz., 1960) said a new pattern must be developed to break a bad habit. The neurons in the brain follow a pattern as behaviours are established that make the task easier to perform. It's hard to break this cycle. To weaken it, you need to create a new habit.

Gradually, the neurons will create a new relationship that becomes a habit when the activity is continuously fostered.

Neuroscientist Elliot Berkman also states that it is safer for the brain to do something different than avoid doing the same task without being replaced.

Start thinking about those changes now if you want any to happen. Expose yourself to materials and educate yourself on the subject. You are thus preparing your subconscious for the transition you are about to launch.

The longer you have the habit, the more difficult it will be to break it.

5.4 Activate the Red Traffic Light in Your Brain

There are two types of cells with approximately equal numbers, one that activates the 'go' signal. One of Duke University's researchers, Nicole Calakos, taught mice to grow behaviours. clicking a button, the mice were trained to get a treat.

They contrasted the educated mice's brains with those of untrained mice and found patterns. They found that there are other 'stop' signals. It is easier for untrained mice to avoid them when their 'stop' warning came first. The trained mice's brains initially triggered the 'go' signal due to the habits they developed.

The go mechanism is powerful when behaviours are repeated and triggered. Reducing activity exposure can slowly decrease the brain's 'go' signal capacity. It's good to break bad habits. The go signal is not reinforced as much when you remember to stop the actions. The habit is low when the go signal does not work regularly.

5.5 They Will Break You or You Break Them

"Cultivate only the behaviours you're able to master." —Elbert Hubbard It can be challenging to alter what you always do and most people don't need to do it. Those who are not easily discouraged will conquer them.

Habits can work for your benefit. They will make you work more quickly. In any task you choose to do, you can be successful.

Yet habits can also harm your growth. To reach their goals, many people are paralyzed; they're letting go of bad habits. We do not practice muscle control that is immune to temptations.

World champions are people willing to sacrifice the comfort they need to win. It can be difficult at the onset to break bad habits. But when you feel the pain and suffering of the workout, you become a winner. You will bounce back and heal the damage caused by bad habits.

If the first attempt doesn't work, that's perfect. Let your mistakes inspire you to redouble your efforts, create new habits, and search for opportunities to better yourself.

You are stronger and more capable of confronting the next step as you resolve your challenges.

Such bad habits are now part of history before you know it. They're no longer getting in your way. They are not enslaving you. They're not dictating your acts.

Instead, you are leading the way.

Hack 4- Keep your willpower and motivation high

Strength does not come with physical capacity. It comes from an indomitable will
\- Mahatma Gandhi

Chapter 6

Concerning a situation or action, achieving our goals is more the product of our daily behaviours than any dramatic circumstance or effort on our part. Habits are a vital part of mind control because your subconscious uses habits as a shortcut or power-saving tool if you use the power of habits to manipulate your mind effectively. Rather than viewing habits as something we need to control and overcome in a negative light, they are an empowering tool to enhance our lives, helping us make changes, thereby making us happy.

To do this, we have to know which habits are good for us, and which habits do not help achieve our goals. Therefore, the first step is to recognize a habit that you want to change for a useful, inspiring, optimistic, good or excellent habit, a new habit you want to develop.

This is a significant step as we are not all conscious of them. We have to take a deliberate look back and recognize the habit or accept that what we tend to do but would like to alter is a repetitive way of reacting.

6.1 Willpower

Now that you know the habit you want to change, do you use your willpower to change it and your motivation to keep it going?

Yes and no. Yes, because both have an essential role to play when it comes to willpower habits and motivation, but they are not enough on their own: there are limitations to be aware of.

Willpower is the power to put will into action to control what you are doing and to restrain yourself. But the thing about will power is that you only have so much of it, and it's hard to rely on it when it runs out – when we are tired, hungry, or sad. That's why you can wake up with a lot of willpower and good intentions, but it's harder to practice your will by evening.

Although the more we do it, the more determination we have to get stronger; and the brain likes your patterns, so it wants to keep them.

So, while willpower has a role to play in improving behaviours, you can't rely on doing it alone. The same applies to inspiration. Think of some habits you've tried to change in the past but couldn't do it and ask yourself honestly why you couldn't? Did you give up on the first sign of trouble? We can never use an excuse in this day and age with so much online information available. Think about it: if you want to lose weight, start a blog, or open a business, all that is required is to Google it, and you'll find thousands of people telling you how to do it step by step. The real reason we don't have what we want is that we are always waiting until we 'feel like doing it,' but the harsh reality is that you will never feel like it. There's no motivation coming, and no one will make you do anything. You've got to do it yourself. Remember the rule of 40% and push yourself past your comfort zone.

You used to think that you will eventually feel like doing something if you want to. You used to think there was going to be inspiration from somewhere. But you'll find that you'll never feel like doing the hard things in life. Think of it: no one ever feels like going on a diet and no one ever feels like getting out of a comfortable warm bed an hour early. If you want to make your ambitions become reality, whether you like it or not, you have to do things. If you're going to make a change in your life, you'll have to do it at the beginning of a new habit you are developing or over any bad habit you want to break. It's going to be hard. It's sudden inspiration and it doesn't last. Emotions are fleeting; they also won't last. Your job is to do the stuff you don't want to do so you can have all you want in life.

We must stop lying to ourselves by saying, 'I'm going to start tomorrow,' because if you don't feel like doing something today, you're not going to feel like doing it tomorrow either.

The difference in those who succeed and unsuccessful people is that they do what's required to get to the goal. The ineffective do what relieves anxiety. Successful people do what they think they ought to do, and whether they like it or not, they act.

Think of muscle endurance. It's accurate until it's gone. When you first start using a muscle, it has a limited amount of endurance, but the more you use it over time, the better it becomes. As Charles Duhigg puts it, 'as people in one part of their lives strengthened their willpower muscles - in the gym or a money management program - that energy was poured into what they ate or how hard they worked. When willpower got stronger, it affected everything. 'That's why it's so effective to make tiny one percent changes. If you are left with VERY little willpower in the tank, you can STILL improve one percent because the perceived difficulty is so low. Therefore, once you go, you will continue to use the 40 percent rule.

You have only one life to live, and you deserve to achieve all you want in life, but if you're waiting to 'feel like it' before you change your bad habits, you'll be waiting forever. As Stephen Guise put it, 'Don't imagine the easiest days when it comes to personal change; imagine the toughest days. If you are tired, stressed, and very busy on the day you can do something; you can do it every day.'

6.2 Motivation

The purpose or 'why' is the motivation behind the new habit you want. Motivation has different levels or layers and different strengths in each. Think of it as condensed circles: circles as in an onion. The outer layer is your significant 'why' or the motivating purpose.

When establishing health and fitness habits, the big motivation of the outer layer is to be healthy and fit as it makes you feel better, gives you more energy, gets you the most out of life, makes you look better as a happier person. It also helps you form better relationships.

You need to develop healthy habits because it feels good to be fit and healthy, making you a happier individual. That's all very well and good, since it's challenging to keep it in the forefront of our minds, and we know that determination will only take us so far, especially when we step into the next layer.

Your condition is the next layer or circle in the onion. For example, you have a busy life, you look after your house, you have a family, a hectic social life, or a lot of commitments, and you're always rushing from one thing to the next.

You arrive at the next layer in which your career or job requires a lot of energy and time from you. Then comes the final layer because a circle represents you right in the middle (like the bullseye on a dartboard). It's written in it the word 'you' of 'me.' This is you when you are talking about this very moment or the present moment.

That's the pattern, but it's not static, because the thickness of these layers varies over days and week; they differ from a Monday morning to the weekend. The idea is your inspiration; it begins with the best of intentions as you pass through the layers.

The morning often starts with good intentions of improving habits; however, you get busy getting breakfast finished and going to work, so the motivation dips and then you in the middle circle – you not so concerned about the broader picture because the needs of the moment are closer to you than the big circle on the outer side. Maybe the needs of the situation are that you're hungry, you're busy and you need something fast to improve your strength; but more importantly to conquer the hunger and do it quickly and easily in a satisfactory way. That's when you don't just focus on willpower and inspiration to support you.

To see what this might be, we need to go back to the idea of what a pattern is. The surprising thing about motivation is that it often comes after starting a new action, not before. We have the common misconception that the consequence of passively watching a motivational video or reading an inspirational book is an inspiration. Active inspiration, however, can be a much stronger motivator.

Motivation is often the outcome of an action, not its cause. Getting started is a type of powerful motivation that naturally generates momentum, even in tiny ways.

Start easy

This phenomenon is referred to as Productivity Physics because it is essentially Newton's First Law applied to habit formation: objects in motion tend to remain in motion. Once a task has started, it is easier to continue moving it forward. Once you have begun a behaviour, you don't need much motivation. Almost all of a task's stress is at the outset. Progress happens more naturally after you start. In other words, completing a job is often simpler than beginning it. Therefore, one of the keys to motivation is to make an easy start.

6.3 How to Get Motivated and Take Action

Most people struggle to find the motivation they need to achieve the goals they want because certain aspects of the process are consuming too much time and energy. If you're going to find motivation easier and get started, it helps to automate your behaviours in their early stages.

Schedule your motivation says Sarah Peck. Many people never get around to writing because they're always wondering when they're going to write next. You can say the same thing about working out, starting a business, creating art, and building most habits.

If exercising doesn't have a time it usually happens, then every day you're going to wake up thinking, 'I hope I feel motivated to practice today'. If your company doesn't have a marketing strategy, then you're going to show up at work crossing your fingers that you're going to find a way to get the word out (in addition to everything else you need to do).

If you don't have a set time to write every week, you'll find yourself saying things like, 'I just want to find the energy to do it'. An article in The Guardian explained the situation: 'If you're wasting resources trying to decide when or where to work, you're going to hinder your ability to do the job.' This makes it simpler for you to follow through, regardless of your level of motivation. And there are plenty of determination and motivation research studies to support this statement.

Stop waiting for your motivation or inspiration to hit you and set a timeline for your behaviours. There is a contrast between amateurs and professionals: professionals set and stick to a timetable, while amateurs wait before they feel motivated or inspired.

6.4 How to be Motivated When You Don't Feel like It

How do some of the world's most prolific artists get motivated? They are not just setting plans; they are creating routines.

Twyla Tharp is widely considered one of the modern era's most celebrated dancers and choreographers. Tharp addresses the role habits or routines of a pre-game have played in her success: She continues a ritual every day of her life; she wakes up at 5:30 a.m., puts on her workout clothes (leg warmers, sweatshirts, and hat). She leaves her Manhattan home, hails a taxi, and tells the driver to take her to the 91st Street Pumping Iron Gym on First Avenue, where she works out for 3 hours. The ritual of stretching and weight training is not what brings her in the gym each morning; the cab is the ritual. The habit is finished the moment she tells the driver where to go.

It's a simple act but performed the same way every morning - making it dull and quick to do. It reduces the chance of skipping it or doing it differently. It's one more thing to worry about in the list of habits, and one less.

Many other well-known creatives have routines. Writer Mason Currey states that many of the world's great artists follow a consistent schedule in the book, Daily Rituals: How Artists Work.

Maya Angelou rented a local hotel room to write. She arrived at 6:30 a.m., wrote to 2:00 p.m., and then went home to edit. At the hotel, she never slept.

Michael Chabon, the recipient of the Pulitzer Prize, writes five nights a week between 10:00 p.m. and 3:00 a.m.

At 4:00 a.m., Haruki Murakami wakes up, writes for five hours, and then goes for a run.

Top creatives' work is not motivated or inspired but follows a consistent pattern and routine. Here are some examples of how ritual and method can be used to get motivated: exercise more consistently and use the same routine in the gym to warm up.

- Make yourself more creative: follow a creative ritual before starting to write or paint or sing.

- Start stress-free every day: create a ritual of meditation for five minutes in the morning.

- Get better sleep: follow the routine of 'powering down' before bed.

A ritual's power, or a pre-game routine, is that it's a mindless way to initiate a behaviour. It makes it easier to start habits, and that means it's easier to keep doing consistently.

The key to any good ritual is to remove the need for decision-making. What should I do first? When do I have to do this? How am I going to do this? Most people never move because they are unable to decide how to get started. You want the behaviour to be comfortable and automatic, so when it becomes difficult and challenging, you have the strength to finish it.

How to Make Motivation a Habit

There are three simple steps to build better routines and make motivation a habit.

Step 1:

Starting with an excellent pre-game routine is so simple that you can't say no to it. To begin your pre-game routine, you shouldn't need motivation. My writing routine, for example, begins with getting a glass of water. My weightlifting routine begins with putting on my lifting shoes. I can't say no to them; these tasks are so simple.

Starting is the most significant part of any task. In the beginning, if you can't get motivated, you will find that motivation always comes after you start. That's why you need to start your pre-game routine incredibly fast.

Step 2:

You can step toward the end goal with your routine. There is often a lack of mental motivation associated with limited or no physical movement. Picture your physical condition when you feel depressed, lonely, or unmotivated. You're not going. You may be slumping over like a glob, melting painfully into the sofa.

The opposite is true, as well. If you're physically moving and involved; you're much more likely to feel mentally engaged and healthy. For starters, when you're dancing, it's almost impossible not to feel lively, awake and energized.

While it should be as easy to start your routine, it should gradually change into more and more physical movement. Your physical movement will follow your mind and motivation. It's worth noting that exercise doesn't have to mean physical movement. For instance, if you aim to write, you should be brought closer to the physical act of writing in your routine.

Step 3:

Every time you have to follow the same pattern. Your pre-game routine's primary purpose is to create a series of events that you always execute before you perform a particular task. The pre-game routine tells the mind, 'This is what's going on before I do.' The routine is embedded in your success such that you're drawn into a mental state that's ready to succeed by merely performing the routine. You don't have to know how to find inspiration; just continue your routine.

You may know that your pre-game routine is essentially making a 'reminder' for yourself. Your pre-game routine is the catalyst that sets off a habit, even though you are not inspired to do it.

This is vital because it's often too much effort to find out what you should do next when you are not motivated. You will often decide just to quit when faced with another decision. However, the solution is the pre-game routine, so you know exactly what to do next. There is no discussion or decision-making. There is no lack of motivation. You're just following the pattern.

How to Stay Motivated for the Long-Run

We've covered a few strategies to make getting motivated and starting a task easier. What about keeping the long-running motivation? How can you be motivated to stay well?

How to Stay Motivated with the Goldilocks Rule

Say you're a tennis player. You'll quickly get bored if you play a serious match against a four-year-old. It's too easy. If you try to play a serious game against a professional tennis player like Roger Federer or Serena Williams on the opposite end of the spectrum, you're likely to become demotivated for another reason: it's too hard.

Compare these encounters to playing tennis with someone you're equal to. You win a couple of points as the game progresses and you lose a couple of points. You've got a chance to win the match, but only if you're trying. Your concentration is narrowing, distractions are fading away, and you are fully committed to the task at hand. The obstacle you face is 'only manageable.' There's no guarantee of success, but it's possible. Science has found that activities like this are the most likely to keep us motivated in the long run.

People like challenges, but only if they are within the optimum difficulty range. There are tedious tasks significantly below your current skills. Tasks that surpass your current capabilities substantially are frustrating. Yet job is right on the edge of success and failure empowers our human brains tremendously. We just want to develop talent beyond the present horizon.

We may call this the Goldilocks phenomenon. The Goldilocks Rule states that when taking on projects on the edge of their current abilities, people experience optimum motivation (Stillam, 2016). Not too complicated. It's not that easy. It's about correct.

One of the keys to retaining long-term motivation is focusing on projects that conform to the Goldilocks rule. If you feel unmotivated to work on a task, it is often because it has drifted into a boredom area or far exceeds your ability. You need to search for a way to pull your tasks back to the limit where you feel challenged but capable.

How to Reach Peak Motivation

Sometimes the beautiful combination of joy and peak output is called flow. Flow is what athletes and performers feel when they're 'in the zone.' Flow is the state of mind you experience when you're so focused on the task that the rest of the world vanishes away.

We might define flow as your highest motivation state in many ways. You'd be stressed to find a time when you're more motivated to take on the job you're working on.

One concern of researchers is whether or not you obey the Goldilocks Rule mentioned earlier. If you are focusing on optimally difficulty tasks, not only will you be inspired, but you will experience a boost in happiness. As psychologist Gilbert puts it, 'One of the major sources of human happiness is working on tasks at an acceptable level of difficulty, neither too hard nor too easy." Moreover, to achieve this peak performance, you need not only to work on challenges at the correct level of difficulty but also assess your immediate progress. One of the keys to entering a flow state, as psychologist Jonathan Haidt states it, is that 'you get instant feedback on how you are doing at each stage.' So we can conclude that evaluation is a crucial factor in motivation. Put it more simply, two of the most critical components of peak motivation are meeting an optimum challenge and getting immediate feedback on the progress you are making towards this goal.

What to do when inspiration eventually drops at some stage: the desire to do a job will slip. If inspiration disappears, what happens? Don't expect to have all the answers, but when you feel like giving up, here's what to remember.

Your Mind is a Suggestion Engine

Consider as a suggestion, not an order, every thought you have. For example, as I'm writing this now, my subconscious says that I'm tired. It suggests that I give up. This may mean that I'll take a more natural path.

But, if I am still in the moment, I will find new ideas. My mind always says that once it's done, I'll feel very good about doing the job. This means that when I stick to the plan, I respect the image I am creating. This means I can complete the mission, even if I don't feel like it. None of these are instructions. They're just options. I can choose which option to follow.

184

Discomfort is Temporary

Compared to the time you spend on your regular day or week, almost any activity you do is done quickly. You'll finish your workout in an hour or two. Tomorrow morning, your message will be typed for completion.

Life is now better than ever before. If you weren't harvesting your food and building your own house 300 years ago, you'd die. Today we whine about our iPhone charger being forgotten.

Keep your perspective. Your life is a great and temporary inconvenience. Step into this uncomfortable moment and let it reinforce you.

Once it's done, it's done. Theodore Roosevelt famously once said, 'Far away, the best prize life has to offer is the opportunity to work hard at work worth doing.' So often it seems we want to work efficiently. We want to be supported and valued in our work, but through it, we don't want to fight. We desire our stomachs to be flat and our arms to be muscular, but if this means doing another workout, we don't want the grind. We want the outcome, but not the preceding failed attempts. In short, we want the gold, but not the grind.

Most want gold medals. Few train like an Olympian. And yet, despite our resistance to it, after the hard work was done, you never felt worse. There are days when starting is damn hard but finishing is always worth it. Sometimes, a victory worth celebrating is the easy act of just showing up. That's half the battle, and then having the courage to do the work accomplishes the full goal when you go all the way.

This is Life

Life is a constant balance between succeeding distractions and overcoming the stress of discipline. It is not an exaggeration to say that in this delicate balance, our lives and personalities are established. What is life if not a multitude of numerous daily battles, small decisions and momentary victories?

The moment when you don't want to do the job is not a moment to throw away. This moment is just as much your life as any other moment. Spend it so you're going to be proud.

Hack 5- Set your Goals

If you want to be happy, set a goal that commands your thoughts, liberates your energy and inspire your hopes.
-Andrew Carnegie

Chapter 7

7.1 What is goal setting?

Many goal-setting exercises begin with an overpaid consultant standing next to a whiteboard and asking something like, What do you see as success? What do you want to do in precise terms? However, if we are serious about our goals, we should start with a very different question. Instead of considering what kind of success we want, we should ask: What kind of pain do I want? This is a strategy I learned from Mark Manson, the author. What Mark found is that it is natural to have a target. Who wouldn't want to write a bestselling book, lose weight, or earn more money? Everyone wants to accomplish these goals.

The real challenge is not to decide if you want the outcome, but to make the compromises necessary to achieve the goal. Would you like the lifestyle of your quest? Would you like the dull and ugly cycle that comes before the glamorous and exciting result?

Sitting around and talking about what we can do or what we would like to do is easy. Accepting the trade-offs that come with our ambitions is an entirely different matter.

It takes us to our first insight into the answer. Goal setting is not just about picking the benefits you want to reap, but also about the cost you're willing to pay.

Rudders and Oars

Imagine a little boat. Your target is like the boat's rudder. They set the course and decide where you're going. If you commit to one goal, the rudder will remain in place, and you will continue to move forward. If you flip-flop between targets, the rudder moves all around, and rowing in circles.

Another part of the boat, however, is even more critical than the rudder: the oars. If your goal is the rudder, the poles will be your way to achieve it. Although the rudder decides your course, your speed is determined by the oars.

The rudder and oars metaphor helps to clarify the distinction between structures and priorities. It is an important distinction that exists everywhere in life.

• Your goal is to win the championship if you're a coach. Every day, the program is what the team is doing in practice.

• If you're an author, you're meant to write a novel. Your routine is the system of writing every week.

• You're running a marathon if you're a runner. Your program will be your monthly training schedule.

• If you're an entrepreneur, creating a million-dollar business is your dream. Your application is your method of sales and marketing.

Objectives are useful in setting the course. Systems are great for making real progress. The most significant advantage of having a target is that it shows you what kind of structure you need to set up. The system itself, however, consists of what the results have been achieved.

This takes us to our second insight into the answer. Goals determine the direction in which you are heading. Programs determine your success. Gripping the rudder, you'll never get anywhere. You've got to row.

7.2 How to Set Goals You'll Follow

Okay, now that we've addressed the trade-offs and structures that come with goals. Now let's think about how you're going to set goals.

There are three basic strategies in setting goals:

1. Ruthlessly eliminate your goals

Psychologists have a term they call 'target rivalry.' Target competition means that the other goals you have are the biggest obstacles to achieving your goals. In other words, for your time and attention, your targets compete with each other. You have to pull focus and energy from your other pursuits whenever you pursue a new goal. This is essentially the theory of the Four Burners in action. You have to turn down the others when you turn one burner up.

There's good news now. One of the great ways to make progress toward your goals is to stop and concentrate on less important things. Sometimes you just need to reorganize your goals a little bit, and instant change comes much quicker as you are now fully committed to a target that had previously received only moderate attention.

This is a valuable insight. Typically, when we don't achieve our goals, we think our goal or approach was wrong. Experts say, You've got to think bigger! Choose a vision that's so huge that it's going to motivate you every day. Or we're thinking, If only I've had more hours in the day! These excuses cloud the more significant issue. What often looks like a goal-setting problem is actually a goal selection issue. It is not bigger goals that we need, but a better focus. You have to choose one thing and do away with everything else ruthlessly. In Seth Godin's words, 'You don't have to take more time, and you just have to know.'

Our lives are like rose bushes. They establish more buds than they can sustain as they grows. If you're talking to an experienced gardener, they'll tell you that you need to prune rose bushes to bring out the best in both their appearance and production. In other words, if you want a rose bush to thrive, then some of the good buds need to be cut off so that the great ones can blossom ultimately.

The priorities are identical. The bushes need to be cut and trimmed consistently. It's natural for new goals to join our lives as we get excited about new opportunities — just like adding new buds is natural for a rose bush. If we can have the confidence to prune a few of our goals, then we will create the space needed to thrive for the remaining goals. Inclusive growth and optimal living need pruning. If you've decided to alter a habit - whether you're quitting smoking, reducing your blood pressure, becoming more involved, or doing something else to improve your health-it is the first step towards making a change.

1. Have your justification

It's imperative to know why you want to change a habit. You may want to stop smoking so that future health problems can be avoided. Perhaps you'd like to eat a healthy diet to lose weight. The purpose may be evident if you have high blood pressure.

To make a change, you need to feel ready. If you're not feeling ready now, that's all right. You can still think and plan. You're prepared for the next step if you want to make a change.

Changing habits is not easy. Yet taking the time to think about what is going to motivate or inspire you will help you achieve your goals.

2. Set goals that you can reach: SMART goals

You've probably already learned about SMART goals. But do you apply the rule at all times? The simple fact is that goals should be built strong to be SMART. Whatever SMART stands for (there are many variants) but the core is that targets should be general.

• Measurable

• Attainable

• Appropriate

• Time-bound

Set Clear Objectives

The goal must be straightforward and well established. Vague or generalised targets are unhelpful, as they do not provide enough guidance. Remember that they show the way; you need goals. Make it as simple as you can by deciding where you want to end up. .

Set Measurable Goals

Include correct numbers, times, and so on for your goals so you can calculate your progress. If your target is described simply as 'Reducing expenses,' how do you know when you've been successful? If you have a one percent reduction in a month, or a ten percent reduction in two years? You will lack the joy that comes with knowing you've achieved something without a way to measure your performance.

Set Realistic Goals

Make sure the goals you set can be accomplished. When you set a goal, you have no hope of achieving; you're just going to demoralize yourself and erode your confidence.

When you are certain about your reasons for wanting to make a change, it's time to set your goals.

- **Long-term targets**: These are the big goals you would like to accomplish in 6 to 12 months.
- **Short-term targets:** What are the short-term priorities that will help you achieve your long-term aims? Short-term objectives are the small steps to improve your health week after week.
- **Revised goals:** Chart your progress and change your goals as you move forward to help you stay motivated.

To set goals, use these tips:

- **Focus on small goals**: This will motivate you overtime to reach larger goals. You're going to have more success with smaller goals, which will help you stay with it.
- **Write down your priorities**: The actual act of writing down a goal makes it concrete and real. You don't have any excuse

to forget that. Use the word 'will' instead of 'would' or 'might' as you write. For example, 'I'm going to cut my operating expenses by ten percent this year, not 'I'd like to cut my operating expenses by ten percent this year.' The first target statement has power, and you can 'see' yourself cutting expenses; the second lacks passion and gives you an excuse if you're side-tracked.

This will help you remember and give you a clearer picture of what you want to do. Use a personal action plan to chart your goals. Hang up your project-plan, and you'll often see it as a reminder of what you're trying to do.

- **Specify your targets**: You will assess your success with specific goals. Setting a target of consuming five fruits and vegetables five days a week, for example, is better than a general goal of' eating more vegetables.' You are less likely to feel stressed and then give up.

- **Reward yourself**: When you reach your goal, celebrate your new behaviour and performance for a few days, and then consider setting your next target.

- **Set Applicable Goals**: Objectives should apply to your life and career path. By having expectations consistent with this, you can grow your concentration and do what you want. Set goals that are common and contradictory, and you're going to squeeze away your time – and your future.

7.3 Prepare for slip-ups

Trying to change a pattern, you go along well for a while, and then have a relapse. It is perfectly normal. Once they reach their goals, many people try and try again.

What are the things that could cause a setback? If you've never tried to change a pattern, think about what has motivated you and what's in the way. Plan by learning about these hurdles now, and how to tackle them if they happen.

There will be a time when you're going to slip up and not make your weekly goal. Don't get frustrated when this happens. Learn from the experience. Ask yourself what's in the way of achieving your goal. When you make lifestyle changes, positive thinking goes a long way.

Stop negative thinking: The more lifestyle changes you have, the easier it is to make those changes.

Seek help with these tips:

- Find a friend: It's motivating to know that another individual also wants to change their lifestyle in the same way, like being more active or altering their eating habits. You've got someone who counts on you to help him, or he succeeds you can remind the person how far they – and you - have come.

- Involve your friends and family: They can work with or encourage you by telling you how they admire what you are doing. With your new healthy eating effort, family members will join in. Don't be afraid to tell your family and friends that their support can make a big difference for you.

- Join a support group or class: Some of the same obstacles plague people in these communities. If you don't feel like sticking to your strategy, they will give you help. When you need a lift, they boost your morale. You can find many support groups online.

- Reinforce yourself positively: Do not waste time feeling bad about yourself when you feel like giving up. Consider why you want to improve, about the strides you've made, and give yourself a pep talk, a pat on the back and a hug.

- Get professional assistance: A registered dietician will help you make healthy choices while still encouraging you to eat the food you love. A trainer or physiotherapist can develop an enjoyable and easy-to-stay exercise program. Your family physician, counsellor, or a social worker will help you to resolve obstacles, reduce stress, or stop smoking.

Healthy eating

Get help when you change your eating habits, so you've chosen to change your eating habits. Good! Have you considered getting support to make this change?

It is an essential part of change to have the support of the people closest to you. If you change careers, a routine, or how you eat doesn't matter as support gives you a better chance to make the change work.

Many people can provide support. Your family and friends can influence the way you eat, but you can also get help from others. There are many types of assistance. Remaining on track can be motivated by constructive words and actions or gentle reminders.

Research shows that it is essential to get support from spouses, family members, and friends to make behavioural changes that affect health. Some people you may expect to support may not help you and may even make it more difficult for you to succeed.

You will determine with whom you would like to discuss your change plans.

- How can you help your family and friends?
- Your family and friends can help you a lot to change the way you live, but you need to discuss it with them.
- Tell your family and friends why this move is being made. Give them reasons and explain why they matter to you.
- Tell them you want their support, but don't expect them to change their lives for you. If they're going to make some of the

same improvements in food as you are, it's perfect. But even without changing the way they feed, they will help you.

Here are a few steps that you and your family can do together for better eating:

- Maintain a regular meal schedule for the family. Families who eat meals together regularly tend to eat healthier foods and stay closer to a healthier weight than those who do not.

- You may be able to discuss some of the same eating changes with your family. This may entail compromise on the part of everybody. It may mean fewer foods and more from others.

- If your diet is different from what your family eats, ask them to eat meals once a week from your food plan. If they see this as pleasant as the food they normally eat, they may choose to eat more of what you choose.

- Installation of a 'no food' policy. Make a food-free room. You can use this space to do stuff you might have done when eating in the kitchen, such as paying bills or helping children with homework. Staying out of the kitchen will help you stick with your food schedule.

- Remove stuff you don't want to consume and place it out of reach. When they have finished eating, remind family members not to leave food on the table.

- Set up a kitchen or refrigerator shelf for healthy foods only. You're going to want several healthy choices when you're hungry.

- Explain the new habit to your children. When you take the kids out once a week for pizza, should you then make a healthier pizza at home? Or you might go out to eat but order the pizza with a salad and other healthy foods. This allows you to fill in other foods in order to eat fewer pizza slices. See if you can find something that everyone can agree on.

- Get support from your friends and family. Ask them not to say negative things about you or what you eat.

- Celebrate with you when you achieve your goals. Take a cooking class or else go to the movies together. Keep reminding yourself and others that you're right.

- To help you make healthy food choices. For example, tell them to help you to eat more fruits and vegetables,

- Encourage you as you slip away from your eating plan. A reminder of how well you have done will help you get back on plan.

- Respect your new habits and they will not urge you to eat foods you don't want to eat.

Most people find that having a friend or food buddy makes the transition easier. A food buddy is someone who is also making changes in his or her eating habits. Learning that someone has the same goals is motivating. Your girlfriend can remind you how far you have come to support you when you have a hard time following your eating plan. For starters, you and your buddy will chat about healthy recipes, ways to prepare regular meals, and how to integrate small amounts of your favourite foods into the food plan.

You may think that friends or family members are doing things that make you feel bad. They don't seem to want you to be good. They may force you to eat more than you like, comment negatively on your new eating habits, and point out how many times you may have messed up.

If this happens, talking to these people is essential. They may not know they're doing it, or that it's upsetting you. Ask them to stop doing it if you need to. You can also ask them why they behave like this.

You may find that they are worried that they will be left out or that you will make them look bad. They may not like the publicity you gain from your change.

If you've decided to start a healthy eating program, making that decision is a significant step towards becoming a healthier person.

Keep these essential points in mind:

- Whether it's healthy eating, getting more exercise, or quitting smoking, you have a better chance of success if you plan ahead.

- Understanding why you want to eat healthier will help your eating habits improve. And if you get discouraged, writing down your reasons will be a good reminder later.

- A plan to develop new habits includes long- and short-term goals as well as strategies to resolve barriers - things that may impede your progress.

- Start with small, short-term goals you can easily reach. Staying with something desired is simpler if you have early, regular achievements.

- Family and friends' encouragement can go a long way to help you achieve healthier eating success. Let them know what you're trying to do and why you are asking for their help.

How are you going to start a healthy eating plan?

It's necessary not to leap in too quickly. You will be ready for success with gradual, steady steps. You will learn the steps to follow in setting up a healthy eating plan:

- Set your goals
- Monitor your development
- Remember the obstacles

• Get help from others and yourself

It's time to set your goals when you're clear about your reasons for beginning a healthy eating program. What is your target for the long term? You want to reach a long-term goal in 6 to 12 months.

Decreasing your blood pressure and/or cholesterol, for example, maybe your long-term goal or reaching a healthy body weight. What are the short-term priorities that are going to get you get there? Short-term goals are things you'd like to do tomorrow and the next day. For example, you may decide to take a low-fat or skim milk or soy beverage instead of whole milk on your cereal to reduce your intake of fat. Or eat fast food once a week or red meat only two times a week.

Some quick tips on healthy eating goals:

- Change your diet plan overnight; instead make your improvements one at a time.

- Instead of taking something away, add something to your diet. Add foods like fruits and vegetables; you need more. You might feel deprived if you start by taking things out of your diet, like foods high in fat or sugar. That will make change more difficult for you.

- Choose more healthy foods you're enjoying. Make a list of the foods you want and see how to make them healthier. For example, use low-fat mozzarella cheese and lots of fresh vegetables to make pizza at home. Do you like a particular raw plant? Stock up on it and reach for it every time you want a snack.

- Write down and hang your goals where you can see them. It can be a helpful reminder to reread your intentions.

- Do not set targets for fast weight loss. Sudden weight loss is not safe, and it is challenging to continue to do.

- Keeping track of your success lets you see how far you have come. It allows you to stick with your strategy as well. Use a diary, log, or food record form to chart the healthy things you're doing. Look at them when you start to doubt or feel discouraged.

Be careful about how you behave. When you eat better, do you notice any difference? Or do you see any difference in eating poorly at times?

Note whether your food preferences are shifting. We learn to like new foods as we change what we consume. You may find that you don't want to eat some of the foods you used to eat before you started making dietary changes. And you might have learned to like new foods you didn't think you wanted.

Take a look at any laboratory tests you may have after you adopted a special diet. You may see changes. Blood sugar checks will tell you if your diet has helped regulate your diabetes. Annual blood tests can assess cholesterol and triglyceride levels.

You should test your blood pressure to see if dietary changes are making it better. If you have high blood pressure, check your blood pressure at home. Reward yourself when you meet your target.

Think about the obstacles. Take your time to think about what might hinder your success. We name these barriers. And by learning about them now, if they happen, you can plan on how to manage them.

Some tips for overcoming barriers:

- Doing something, stopping it, and then getting mad at yourself is perfectly normal. Once they reach their goals, many people have to try and try again.

- Don't forget little bonuses, something to look forward to keep you going.

- Expect obstacles to be identified. And remember that the goal is not to remove barriers, but to identify them in advance and prepare what you are going to do to overcome them.

- It may help to have a written personal action plan listing your goals, obstacles, and strategies to resolve those barriers.

And get support - from others and yourself. It will be easier to change your eating habits, the more help you have. If your family members tell you they love how healthy you are, you're going to be motivated to keep up the excellent job.

And out there's more help. You can even ask for incentives. Looking for a few things: don't forget to repay yourself. Give yourself a treat when you hit one of your targets - eating five portions of fruits and vegetables a day for one week, for example.

Purchase a safe cookbook for yourself. Take a class of cooking. Or just take yourself a little time. Do everything it takes to reassure yourself that your targets have been achieved. You have reached it!

Hack 6- Implementation and Measuring

Be creative while inventing ideas, but be disciplined while implementing them
- Amit Kalantri

Chapter 8

Stack Your Goals

Evidence has shown that if you make a specific plan for when, where, and how you execute an action, you are two to three times more likely to stick to your goals. For example, in a study, scientists asked people to address this sentence: 'I will engage in at least 25 minutes of vigorous exercise on [DAY] at [TIME OF DAY] at/in [PLACE] during the next week.' Researchers found that individuals who filled out this sentence were more likely to exercise as compared to that group that did not make plans for their future behaviour. Psychologists call these specific plans 'implementation expectations' as they specify when, where, and how a particular activity is to be enforced. This result have been replicated across hundreds of studies. It has shown to increase the chances that people will continue to exercise, start recycling, stick with learning, and even stop smoking.

The best way to use this finding is adopt or stack the habit of a strategy call. To use habit stacking, simply fill in this phrase: for example, I will [NEW HABIT] after / Before [CURRENT HABIT].

Here are some examples:

- Meditation: I'm going to meditate for a minute after I brew my morning coffee.
- Push-ups: I'm going to do ten push-ups before taking my morning shower.
- Flossing: I'm going to floss my teeth after I put my toothbrush down.
- Gratitude: I'm going to say one thing I'm thankful for before I eat dinner.
- Networking: I will send an email to someone after I get back from my lunch break.

Habit stacking works well because you're not only making a specific plan for when and where to achieve your goals, but you're also linking your new goals to something you're doing every day. Researchers think this is a useful way of bridging the gap between goals and systems. The goals tell us what we want to do while the mechanism we implement every day is the process. Habit stacking and executing goals help us move to the specific process that will make the target in our heads a reality.

8.1 Set the Upper Bound

We almost always concentrate on the lower bound when we set goals. I'm speaking of the minimum threshold we're going to hit. The implicit assumption is, 'Yeah, if you can do more than the minimum, go for it.'

- An individual may say, 'This month, I want to lose at least 5 pounds.'
- An entrepreneur might say, 'Today, I want to make at least ten sales calls.'
- An author could say, 'Today, I want to write at least 500 words.'
- A basketball player could say, 'Today, I want at least 50 free throws.'
- You could say:
- 'I want to lose at least 5 pounds this month, but not more than 10.'
- 'I want to make at least 10 sales calls today, but not more than 20.'
- 'I want to write at least 500 words today, but not more than 1,500.'
- •' I want to make at least 50 free throws today, but not more than 100.'

To make progress, you want to push hard enough, but not so much that it is unsustainable. This is where it may be beneficial to set an upper limit. Upper limits make it simpler for you to keep up with your success.

In the beginning, this is particularly critical. The most significant thing is to show up anytime you set a new target and start working towards it. At first, showing up is even more important than succeeding because if you don't develop the habit of showing up, then in the future, you will never have anything to change.

How to achieve your Goals consistently

Good goal setting allows the structure that surrounds us to be addressed. Too often, within the wrong system, we set the right goals. If we fight the order every day to make progress, then making consistent progress will be hard.

There are all sorts of hidden forces that make it easier or more challenging to achieve our goals. Our worlds must be consistent with our goals.

8.2 How to Align Your Environment with Your Goals

While most of us at any given time have the freedom to make a broad range of choices, we sometimes make decisions based on the world in which we find ourselves. For instance, if you wanted to write a guide, you might drink a beer. You could be sitting at your desk with a glass of water next to you, though. No beers in sight. While you can get up, walk to the car, drive to the supermarket, and buy a beer, you probably won't because easier alternatives surround you. In this situation, the default decision is to take a sip of water - an easy decision.

Similarly, the choices that surround us form many of the decisions we make in our professional and personal lives. When you sleep with your phone next to your pillow, the default decision is likely to check social media and emails as soon as you wake up.

When you step into your living room, and all of your couches and chairs are facing the TV, watching the screen is possibly the default choice.

When you have alcohol in your house, the default choice is to drink regularly.

Defaults can also be optimistic, of course. When you have a dumbbell next to your desk at work, it is more likely to be the default choice to churn out some fast curls. When you carry a water bottle with you throughout the day, the default option is more likely to be drinking water rather than soda. When you put floss in a visible location (like your toothbrush), the default choice is more likely to be flossing.

Scientists refer to the effect that defaults on the world can have as the architecture of choice on decision-making. This has a significant impact on achieving goals. Whether or not you reach your long-term goals has a lot to do with what kinds of forces surround you in the moment. In a negative environment, it is tough to stick to good behaviours.

Here are a few strategies that I found useful in for life when trying to design better default decisions for simplicity. When you are constantly surrounded by noise, it's hard to focus on the signal. If the kitchen is filled with junk food, it is harder to eat well. When you have ten tabs open in your desktop window, it's harder to concentrate on reading a blog post. If you slip into the illusion of multitasking, it is harder to accomplish the most crucial task. Eliminate the choices in question.

Placing products on eye-level shelves in the store makes them more recognisable and more likely to be purchased. You can use visual signals like the Paper Clip System or the Seinfeld Strategy outside the store to create an environment that subtly nudges the acts in the right direction.

Opt-out or opt-in.

There is a modern study of organ donation that showed how many European countries have skyrocketed their rates of organ donation: they wanted people to opt-out of donation rather than opt-in. In your life, you can do something similar by choosing your future self ahead of time through better habits. For example, you might schedule your next week's yoga session when you feel motivated today. You have to justify opting-out instead of motivating yourself to opt-in when your workout rolls around.

8.3 Measure Your Goals

Measurement is another secret to the long-term success of your goals. The human mind is fond of receiving feedback. Proof of success is one of the most inspiring things we can encounter. That's why measurement is so critical to setting goals effectively. You gain insight into whether or not you are making progress by evaluating performance. The things we are measuring are those we are improving. If we get better or worse, it is only through numbers and simple monitoring that we have some idea.

Here are some of the measurable goals:

I got stronger when I measured how many pushups I've made.

I read more books while I recorded my 20-page reading habit a day.

I started to live with more integrity when I recorded my values.

The trick is to understand that it is not specifically about the outcome to count, weigh, and track. Moreover, it is a means of learning, finding out, and knowing. Test to see if you're present. Check to see if the things that are important to you are spending time.

8.4 Measure Backward, Not Forward

When looking ahead, you measure progress. You're setting goals. For success, you schedule milestones. Ultimately, to some extent, you are trying to predict the future.

In industry, wellness, and life as a whole, ask this.

- Is it possible to increase your quarterly earnings by 20%?

- In the next three months, will you lose 20 pounds?

- Going to be married at 30?

These are all forward-looking calculations. You're looking ahead trying to guess when you're going to get somewhere. There's a different approach, and more useful: calculate backwards, not forward.

Measuring backward vs measuring forward

Sit down at your computer every week and fill out a little spreadsheet to chart your business' critical metrics: traffic, subscribers to email, sales, expenditures, etc. By now, you've been down the road pretty often, so it only takes about 15 minutes.

However, you get straightforward input in those 15 minutes as to whether or not you are making progress in the areas that matter most. You can tell the way things are moving. And, if the numbers shift the wrong way in one week, the following week, you can make adjustments.

Essentially, you calculate backward progress (what happened this week in your business?) and use back calculation as a way to direct your next week's acts. In the gym, you can use a similar strategy: each Tuesday, Thursday, and every Friday, open your journal when you arrive to look at the weights you lifted during your last or two workouts. So, by marginally increasing the sets, reps, or weight from where they were from last week, you schedule your workout. Of course, you are looking for small increases. You are interested in the return of one percent.

You calculate backwards in the gym, just like in your company, and use that calculation to decide your next move. You are still looking for improvement, but you base your decisions on what has happened recently, not on what you think will happen in the future.

The habit chains are too weak to feel until they are too strong to be broken.

Samuel Johnson said one of our greatest struggles is to keep aware of what we are doing when it comes to building good habits and breaking bad habits. The more a behaviour becomes automatic, the less likely it is to be noticed. This helps to explain how we can be sneaked into the consequences of bad habits. By the time we consider the consequences of our decisions, we are already dependent on the new behaviour pattern.

Measuring backwards, however, will draw attention to these unseen patterns by making you conscious of what you are doing. Measuring backwards allows you to consider your recent actions. You can't live in a world of hopes and dreams like in a fairy tale. You need to look at what has happened recently in your life and then base your choices and changes on these data bits.

The news is that you can make your decisions on what you are currently doing, not on what you are hoping to do for your future self.

The importance of short-term feedback

'The best way to improve long-term behaviour is with short-term feedback.' —Seth Godin. This approach has one caveat: the data needs to come from the recent past when you calculate backwards.

If you used data to assess progress and make business decisions two years ago, your choices would have been off. The same applies to weightlifting or other areas of improvement. You don't want decisions to be focused on what you have done long ago, but on what you've recently achieved. In other words, you want to input in the short term, not in the long term - the better, the quicker.

Measuring for satisfaction

This approach has an additional benefit. When you calculate backwards, you will be able to enjoy the change you are making now rather than looking forward to a new life in the future.

Once you hit a potential milestone or goal, you don't have to put off your joy. Happiness in the future is no longer the endgame out there. Focusing on how you can improve your past self in the immediate future is more satisfying than comparing your current state to where you hope to be someday.

Put the idea into practice

Almost every improvement you want to make in your life requires some kind of change in behaviour. You have to do something differently if you want different results. The hard question to answer is, what are you expected to do differently to get the results you want?

You tend to react by focusing on an outcome and setting a target. Goals are excellent, and it's essential to have a sense of direction to where you want to go. Yet calculating backwards is the way to go when it comes to determining the changes you can make right now. Let the recent results guide your actions in the future. For example:

Weight loss: test your intake of calories. Last week, did you eat 3,500 calories a day? Based this week, on an average of 3,400 per day

Strength Training: well, you squatted 250 pounds last week for five sets of 5 reps? Give this week a try of 255 pounds.

Relationships: last week, how many new people have you met? If zero, then reflect on this week's introduction to a new individual.

Entrepreneurship: although your average is five, you landed just two customers last week? It sounds like this week; you're going to focus on making further sales calls.

Measure backwards and get a bit better afterwards. What have you been doing last week? How can you change this week just a bit?

8.5 The Seinfeld Strategy

Seinfeld said the way to be a better comic is to create better jokes and the way to create better jokes is to write jokes every day. He got a big wall calendar and hung it on the wall for a whole year. A big red magic marker was his next move. He said, '[I'll do my writing assignment for every day; I'll put a big red X over that day.'

You're going to have a chain after a few days. Just hold on to it, and every day the chain will grow longer. You'll love to see that chain, especially if you get under your belt for a couple of weeks. Your only duty is not to break the chain.

You will notice that Seinfeld hasn't said a single result thing. Whether he was inspired or not, it didn't matter. It didn't matter whether or not he wrote great jokes. It didn't matter if it ever make it into a series he was working on. And that's one of the clear truths behind the incredible success and continuity of Seinfeld.

How to stop procrastinating by using the Seinfeld Method

Top performers in all sectors - athletes, singers, CEOs, artists - are all more reliable than their peers. Day after day, they wake up and deliver while everyone else gets stuck with the urgencies of everyday life and fights a constant battle between procrastination and motivation.

While most people get demotivated and off-track after a poor performance, a bad workout, or just a bad day at work, the next day, top performers settle back into their routine.

The Seinfeld Strategy works because it helps to shift focus away from each performance and puts emphasis on the process. It's not about how you look, how motivated you are, or the beauty of that day's work. Instead, it's just about 'not breaking the chain.' All you have to do is pick up a calendar and launch your chain to apply this technique to your own life.

A Word of Note

The Seinfeld Strategy has one drawback. You have to choose a job important enough to make a difference, but it's easy enough to get it completed. If you could write ten pages a day for your book, it would be great, but it's not a sustainable chain to create. Likewise, in theory, it sounds great to be able to raise the dead like a man every day, but in reality, you are likely to be overstrained and burned out.

Step one is, therefore, to choose a job that is sufficiently easy to be sustainable. At the same time, you must ensure that your acts are sufficiently relevant to the matter.

Looking for good jokes every day, for example, is easy, but you will never write a joke just by researching. This is why the writing process is a better choice. Writing, even when performed in small doses, will produce a meaningful result.

Likewise, it could be useful and straightforward to do ten pushups per day, depending on your fitness level. It will make you stronger. Moreover, it's simple to read a fitness book every day, but it won't get you in better shape.

Pick tasks that are easy to maintain and capable of achieving the desired outcome. Another way of saying this is to focus on actions and not motions. Consider the concept: mistakes smart people master follow consistency.

The central question that binds our community together - and what you are trying to write about every Monday and Thursday - is, 'How do you live a healthy life?' It involves not just nutrition and exercise, but discovery and adventure, art and imagination, and culture and connection.

But they all need consistency, no matter what topic you are talking about. No matter what your definition of a 'healthy life' is, to make it a reality, you will have to fight procrastination. Ideally, the Seinfeld Strategy will help bring this war into perspective.

Don't break your exercise chain, and you'll quickly find that you're getting fit. Don't split the business chain, and you're going to find the results are coming much quicker. Do not break the chain of your artistic pursuits, and you will find that you are continually generating creative work.

Believe that success takes a monumental effort and that your lofty goals require enormous amounts of determination and inspiration. Al you need is to commit yourselves to small, manageable tasks. Mastery is the result of consistency.

8.6 Why and How to Track Ultimate Habit Tracking

Maintaining a habit tracking is one easy and useful thing you can do if you want to stick to a habit for good. Here's why: top performers also chart their success, measure it, and report it in different ways. Every small calculation enables feedback. It sends a signal as to whether progress is being made or whether changing direction is required.

Gabrielle Hamilton, a New York City chef, is a good example. During an interview, she said, 'The one thing I see is that the chef is constantly separated from the home cook is that we taste everything, all the time, right down to the salt grains, before we apply it to the pan. We slurp olive oil glasses and aerate them in our mouths as if it was a wine that we tried to know.'

The Habit Tracker: what is it and how does it works

A habit tracker is an easy way to measure if you've made a habit. The most basic method is to get a calendar and stick to your schedule every day. For instance, if you meditate on Monday, Wednesday, and

Friday, you get an X for each of those dates. The calendar will become a record of your habit streak as time goes by.

Develop a Habit Journal containing twelve habit tracker templates, one for each month to make this process as easy as possible. All you need to do is add your habit and start to cross off the days.

The classic approach is to put an X on each day. If you are a little more design-oriented, on your habit tracker, you can shade in the cells. You can also use checkmarks or fill your habit tracker with dots. The key point here is that your habit tracker gives clear evidence that you have achieved the habit. It's a symptom that progress is being made. Of course, that's not all it does.

There are three reasons why habit tracking is strong:

- It provides a visual cue for you to act.
- Seeing the progress you are making is inspiring. You don't want your string to end.
- Recording your success at the moment feels rewarding.

Let's break down every single one.

Advantage #1: You are prompted to behave by a habit tracker.

Naturally, habit tracking builds a series of visual indications. You'll be reminded to act again when you look at the calendar and see your streak.

Studies have shown that people who monitor their progress on goals such as weight loss, smoking cessation, and lowering blood pressure are all more likely to increase success than those that don't. A survey of over 1600 people found that those who maintained a daily food log lost twice weight as those who did not. A habit tracker is a simple way of recording your actions and monitoring a pattern that will trigger the urge to change it.

Tracking your habits keeps you accountable, as well. Most of us say that we are doing better than others. Measurement offers one way of overcoming our blindness to our behaviour and noticing what's going on every day. You will not lie to yourself when the evidence is right in front of you.

Advantage #2: You are encouraged to proceed with a habit tracker.

Progress is the most effective motivation. We become more motivated to continue to the path when we get a signal that we are moving forward. Tracking habits can have an addictive impact on motivation in this way: every little victory feeds your desire.

On a bad day, this can be especially powerful. When you're feeling down, all the progress you've already made is easy to forget. Tracking your habit offers visual evidence of your hard work and a subtle reminder of how far you have come. Plus, the empty square you see every morning will motivate you to get started because by breaking your streak, you don't want to lose your progress.

Advantage #3: A habit tracker gives instant gratification.

Eventually, it is easy to watch. Crossing an item off your to-do list, completing an entry in your workout log, or marking an X on the calendar is satisfactory. Watching your performance grow is good, and you are more likely to survive.

Habit monitoring also helps keep your eye on the ball: you focus more on the system than on the result. You're not going to get six-pack abs; you're just trying to keep the streak alive and become the type of person who does not skip workouts.

Ideas and benefits sound great, but you don't have to fill your habit tracker with any habits that make up your day. Yes, if you're already sticking to a routine, then monitoring it as well seems like extra work. So what is your habit tracker going to measure?

Habit monitoring will help you set off a new habit or keep track of habits you tend to forget or slip when things get busy. It is recommended to use the Two-Minute Rule from Atomic Behaviours, which recommends you scale down your behaviours until two minutes or fewer are required to execute them. You can log whatever habits you want in your habit tracker, but it is suggested to start with these super-small habits to make sure you show up every day, at least in a small way.

See the examples below and split them out into daily, weekly, and monthly patterns.

A widespread daily habit of tracking:

- journal one sentence
- one minute push up
- stretch for one minute
- write one thing that makes me happy
- make the bed
- wake up by [TIME]
- go to bed by [TIME]
- take a shower
- floss my teeth
- weigh myself
- take medication
- take vitamins/supplements
- play [INSTRUMENT] for one minute
- touch one potential customer
- prioritize my to-do list
- say 'I love you' at least once
- put all the dishes away
- take a walk

- call mother
- walk the dog

Note that most things on this list take a minimum of one minute to two. Make your habits so easy that even on the tough days, you can stick to them.

You need to repeat the list frequently to make something genuinely habitual. As a result, the bulk of activities are every day. But using a habit tracker for different weekly or monthly routines can also be helpful. Behaviours, like tying your shoes or brushing your teeth, will not become 'automatic,' but a habit tracker can still remind you to complete them.

Popular weekly habits to track:

- publish a blog post
- vacuum
- take out the trash/do recycling
- do laundry
- water plants
- clean up bedroom
- write a thank-you note
- check finances
- transfer money to savings account
- pay off credit cards
- pay deep clean house bills

You can also use a habit tracker to count how often you do something simple. For instance, you may want to keep track of how many days you travel each month for work. Consider.

- days spent travelling

- perform daily reviews
- perform monthly reviews

You can use a behaviour tracker to monitor what you are not doing. These are called 'evasion patterns' (that is, activities that you try to avoid). See our website for free downloadable resources

Good new habits:

- no alcohol
- no Netflix
- no buying online
- no soda
- no sugar
- no caffeine
- no smoking

The Habit Journal provides a proven template and the fastest way to create your habit tracker. No need to draw your grid for an hour. Simply write down your routines, and you're good to go.

Get used to using your Habit Tracker

With all the advantages of using a habit tracker, however, it isn't something that makes sense in every circumstance or for individual. Many people oppose the notion of monitoring and measuring. It may feel like a challenge because it pushes you into two habits: the habit you try to build and the habit of observing it. That said, almost anyone in one way or another can benefit from habit tracking, even if it is only temporary.

Can we do to make it easier to track habits?

The most critical activities should be limited to manual monitoring. It is easier to track one habit continuously than to track ten sporadically. Keep your habit tracker easy and limit it to three or four major habits.

Immediately after the habit occurs, record the calculation. The habit's completion is the prerequisite to writing it down. (This is a variation on the 'habit piling' strategy. Here's the basic formula: I'll [TRACK MY HABIT] after [CURRENT HABIT].

For example:

- mark the column 'call one potential client' after hanging up the phone from a sales call.

- fill the column 'meditate for one minute' after you finish meditating.

- After putting your plate in the dishwasher, finish the line 'clean all the dishes.'

The practice of using the habit tracker is what we're talking about here. These little rules will help you remember to pick up your habit tracker and mark another achievement.

Quick recovery when your habits break down

Finally, when you fall off the wagon at some point, every habit strike stops. Perfection cannot be accomplished. An emergency is coming up soon: you get sick, or you have to travel for work, or your family needs a little more time. Try to remind yourself of a simple rule when this happens: never miss it twice.

Hack 7- Meditation

Meditation is a process of lightening up, of trusting the basic goodness of what we have and who we are, and of realizing that any wisdom that exists in what we already have. The key is to wake up, to become more alert, more interested and curious about ourselves
- Pema Chodron

Chapter 9

Habitual patterns limit our options and hold us hostage. Our thoughts and emotions default to a usual response due to the tendencies we create out of habit. Without awareness, we dig into our minds ever deeper grooves: habitual behaviour patterns that can either be positive or negative. Through the practice of awareness, we can start to see this process and disrupt it over time.

It can be present for just one moment every time we have thought that arises and goes by, or we can repeat it to ourselves over and over again. For me, it's like water; it can go anywhere if you pour a drop on the earth. But if that drop begins to take some path, and the next drops follow, the water will make a groove after a while.

Each time a drop goes down that path, it creates a deeper rhythm, and the choices are becoming increasingly limited. Meditation awareness leads to more mental freedom; the knowledge we gain in meditation is a way to get us back to square one, where the water now has options to flow.

Consciousness is the key to solving the issues that our normal responses bring. Let's take recurring fears as an example. We may have been in or witnessed a car accident, so we react in some way whenever we think of a 'car.' And every time we have this reaction, we intensify the rhythm so that we have the same reaction the next time the stimulus occurs. But with awareness, we understand what is happening at the moment so that each time an event happens, new knowledge is generated. Every time we get a little faster understanding.

Eventually, the very moment it arises, we find ourselves recognizing our usual tendency. This is the moment we have different possibilities. The water doesn't have to go down the same channel because we're at a place where different ways can steer a dropping drop. We know that we've got options. The deeper our practice of mindfulness, the greater our independence and ability to understand and work with our impulses.

We can apply this practice to the usual tendencies with family members, difficult co-workers, etc. that always seem to abound. Typically, our leanings determine our reactions because we don't know about them and often capture them too late – if at all. We've been swept away without awareness, since we've already reacted. Everything was going too fast; we didn't catch it in time. But with awareness, the moment it manifests, we can see our tendency and change our response to something more workable, and more beneficial. The ideal technique is meditation. If we develop the powerful habit of returning to the breath in meditation when something occurs midstream, we keep our awareness in all kinds of situations. We've disrupted the usual pattern, and now the water has a new place to go.

Events get out of control when certain factors are present. And it's just because of the knowledge that things are dwindling back to normal. They are falling back into proportion, and with what is going on, we can have a more balanced and healthy relationship. We are also cultivating a kind of trust in resting with the breath, along with awareness. Try it and see for yourself the subtle changes it makes. You can keep it in your pocket once you've had the experience and use it when you're in a usual 'trigger' situation.

It doesn't only happen on the cushion

Meditation is not something that only happens on the cushion. When we're sitting, there's awareness, focus, and presence; but there's no reason they can't be there every moment of your life. When intense situations happen and create fear, anxiety, or conflict, you're usually likely to be swept away. But actually, because it's such an intense experience, and so in your face, tagging it and reacting differently is easier for you!

Subtle thoughts and worries are equally bad habits, and they are harder to work with because they appear to be hidden. You don't see them since it's the big things that bring you back to your preparation and remind you that you can use this device, this gift, or good practice to improve your experience. When you change your experience, you change the entire situation effectively. It may not be 100 percent of the time, but because you are aware, your reactions can potentially be more measured and healthier. Between behaving with indifference and acting with knowledge, there is a vast difference

Steps for meditation

1. Sit comfortably on a chair, your feet on the floor, and your hands on your thighs. (You can sit on the floor if you prefer.) Take two or three deep breaths and close your eyes.

2. Starting from the top of your head and moving down, scan your body mentally, noticing any tension in your muscles, places of comfort or discomfort, while feeling the floor under your feet. Start paying attention to your breath's natural rhythm.

3. Follow the rising and falling sensation without changing it in any way, silently counting breaths as you become more conscious of your breath.

Inevitably, your mind will wander. This is one of the first lessons of meditation. When you notice that you've been distracted by a thought, let go of it and give your attention back to your breath. You're going to learn to step back over time and just watch the views. The same applies to sounds: let them come and go instead of trying to block them out.

4. Take a few seconds to allow your mind to do whatever it wants. (You may find your mind is tranquil.) Realizing the sounds around you and putting your attention back to the body, slowly open your eyes.

When to do it: many people meditate the first thing in the morning, to start the day with a clear head, but everybody's different, so find what works for you.

How often: the more you practice, the sooner you will see benefits, but consistency matters more than quantity, so concentrate on 'small and often,' taking the time to build a strong base. If every day sounds like too much at first, continue with three to five days a week.

How long: for beginners, just ten minutes a day will suffice. (Use a timer or an app, so you didn't have to watch the clock.) For some people that has always been enough, but ultimately you may decide to sit for more extended periods, especially once you begin to feel the wonderfulness of your newfound headspace.

Tricks to Make New Habits Stick

Creating better jokes was the way to be a better comedian, so write better jokes every day
- Seinfeld

Chapter 10

Pick up a big wall calendar and hang it all year round on a common wall. The next pass was a big red magic marker. Seinfeld said that daily I'm going to do my writing assignment; every day, I'm going to put a big red X.

You're going to have a chain after a couple of days. Just hang on to it, and the chain will grow longer every day. You're going to love seeing that chain, particularly if you get under your belt for a couple of weeks. Your effort is not to break the chain.

It didn't matter if he was inspired or not. Whether or not he wrote great jokes didn't matter. If he ever turned it into a collection of what he was working on, it didn't matter.

And this is one of the simple facts behind Seinfeld's incredible success and continuity.

Let's talk about not procrastinating in your life using the Seinfeld Process

How to avoid procrastinating

Top performers in all fields - athletes, actors, CEOs, musicians - are all more efficient than their peers. They get up and deliver day after day while everyone else gets stuck with daily life's urgencies and fights a constant battle among procrastination and motivation.

Most people get demotivated and off-track due to poor performance, a bad workout, or just a bad day at work, top performers settle back into their routine the next day. The Seinfeld Strategy works because it helps shift focus away from every event and focuses on the process. It's not about how you look, how you're motivated, or the beauty of the work of that day.

You have to pick up a calendar and start your chain to apply this technique to your own life.

A word of note

One drawback to the Seinfeld Strategy. You have to choose work sufficiently important to make a difference, but simple enough to complete . It would be great if you could write ten pages a day for your book, but it's not a sustainable chain. Likewise, it sounds great in theory to be able to raise the dead like a man every day, but you're likely to be overstrained and burned out.

Thus, step one is to choose a career that is easy to sustain. At that time, you have to make sure your actions are important enough to matter. For example, it's easy to look for good jokes every day, but you're never going to write a joke just by researching. That's why it is a better choice to write. Writing will produce a meaningful result, even if done in small doses.

Depending on your fitness level, it could also be easy and useful to do ten pushups a day. It's going to make you happier. It's also easy to read every day a fitness novel, but it won't get you in better shape.

Choose tasks that are easy to maintain and able to achieve the desired result.

Another way to say this is to concentrate on acts rather than movements, which is the idea discussed in my article: Mistake That Smart People Make Mastery Follows Consistency.

The central question that ties our society together, and what I'm trying to write about every Monday and Thursday is, 'Where do you live a healthy life' But they all need to be consistent, regardless of the topic we are addressing. Regardless of what your idea of normal life is, you'll have to fight procrastination to make it a reality. Ideally, this conflict will be put into perspective by the Seinfeld Strategy.

Don't break the chain of exercise, and you'll soon find that you're getting fit. Don't break the company chain, and the results will come much quicker. Do not break the chain of your artistic pursuits, and you will find that creative work is continuously being produced.

So often, we conclude that success requires a monumental effort and that our lofty goals require a great deal of dedication and motivation. But all we need is to engage in small, manageable tasks. The result of consistency is mastery.

Maintaining a habit monitoring is one simple and useful thing you can do if you want to stick to a habit for good.

Here's why: top performers are also charting, calculating, and recording their performance in different ways. Every little measurement provides feedback. This sends a signal as to whether progress is being made or whether it is necessary to change direction.

A good example is Gabrielle Hamilton, a chef from New York City. She said during an interview with the New York Times, 'The one thing I see is that the chef is always isolated from the home cook is that we taste everything, all the time, right down to the salt grains, before adding it to the pan. We slurp olive oil glasses and aerate them in our mouths as if it were a wine we wanted to learn.'

10.1 How to Stick With Good Habits Every Day by Using the "Paper Clip Strategy"

Additional Tricks

A bank in Abbotsford, Canada hired a stockbroker named Trent Dyrsmid, a twenty-three years old, in 1993. Abbotsford was a relatively small suburb tucked in neighbouring Vancouver's shadow, where most of the big business deals were made. Nobody expected too much of him because of the position and the fact that Dyrsmid was a rookie. Yet, thanks to a simple daily routine, he made brisk progress.

The Paper Clip Strategy

Dyrsmid began with two jars on his desk every morning. One was loaded with 120 clips. The other was empty. He would make a sales call as soon as he settled in every day. He would move a paper clip from the full jar to the empty jar immediately afterwards, and the process would start again. 'I'd start with 120 paper clips in one jar every morning, and I'd keep dialling the phone until I moved all of them to the second jar,' he said.

Dyrsmid contributed $5 million to the organization within eighteen months. He made $75,000 a year by the age of twenty-four, the equivalent of $125,000 today. Not long after, he found another business with a six-figure salary.

The Tale of Trend: better habits that last vs habits that fail

When asked about his habit's specifics, Dyrsmid just said, I'd start calling at 8:00 a.m. Every day. He never looked at quotations from securities or analysis from analysts. He never read the newspaper all the time. If the news was relevant, it would reach him from other directions.

Dyrsmid is proof of a simple truth: success is often the result of constant dedication to the fundamentals. Compare Trent's results with where we often find you. We want our routines to be regular, but we're struggling to make it into the gym. What's the difference? While others break, why do some good habits stick? Why has the paper clip technique of Trent performed so well, and what can we learn from it?

The "Paper Clip Strategy" works particularly well with the Power of a Visual Flash because it provides a visual cue that helps motivate us to practice a behaviour more regularly. It is learned from writers who use it in a variety of ways. For example, as she wrote a page in her novel, one woman moved a hairpin from one jar to another. After every set of push-ups, another man moved a marble from one bin to the next.

It is rewarding to make progress, and visual steps such as moving paper clips or hairpins or marbles provide clear evidence of success. As a result, they improve our actions and bring to any task a little bit of immediate satisfaction.

Here are a few reasons why visual indicators work well to create new good habits. Visual indications encourage us to continue a practice. You lie about your ability to remember executing a new habit, like 'I'm going to start eating better. For real this time.' But, a few days later, the inspiration fades, and life's business begins to take over again. Making a new habit is usually a recipe for failure. That's why a visual stimulus can be so beneficial, like a bin full of paper clips. When your environment pushes you in the right direction, it's much easier to stick to good habits.

Physical signs show your improvement. Everybody recognizes that consistency is an essential component of success, but in fact, few people calculate how reliable they are in real life. The Paper Clip Strategy avoids this pitfall because it is an integrated measuring system. One look at your clips of paper and you have a sense of your success instantly.

Visual signs can have a motivational effect that is addictive It is normal to become more motivated to continue the habit as the visible evidence of progress mounts. The more paper clips you put in the jar, the more inspired you become to complete the task. Many current studies in behavioural economics refer to this as the Endowed Progress Effect, which essentially says that once you have them, you place more value on items. That is, the more paper clips you move to the 'completed' jar, the more valuable it becomes for you to complete the habit.

Physical cues can be used to boost motivation in the short and long term. The technique of the paper clip provides everyday inspiration, yet every day you start from scratch. Another form of visual cue, however, such as the 'don't break the chain' calendar mentioned, can be used to highlight the consistency over extended periods. You can create a set of visual signals by putting these two approaches together to inspire and monitor your patterns.

Creating your paper clip strategy

There are many ways to use the paper clip technique to accomplish goals. Would you like to do 100 pushups every day? Start with ten clips of paper and push one over each drop and do a set of 10 all day long.

Do you need to send 25 emails each day? Start with 25 clips, and each time you press 'Send', toss one to the other side.

Would you like to drink eight glasses of water every day? Start with 8 clips, and each time you finish a bottle, slide one over.

If you'd like to take a prescription three times a day, set 3 paper clips out each time you swallow your pills and drop one into the jar; it will cost you less than $10 for the entire strategy.

Take a box of standard paper clips. Choose two regular holders and start moving the bad guys from side to side. Trent Dyrsmid determined that one of his key tasks was to attain success in his field: making more calls for sales. He discovered that what makes the difference is to learn the fundamentals.

The same applies to your targets.

- There's no secret sauce
- There's no magic bullet
- The magic ingredient is good habits

10. 2 Make a Commitment to Your Self

It takes conscious thinking and planning to commit to forging good habits. In everything you do in life, either you honour your sacred self, or you don't. To achieve all this, there is a key step in transforming habits, preparing yourself mentally for a small action, and overcoming any obstacles thrown in your way.

'Do not concentrate on doing behaviour X. Rather, focus on making behaviour X easier to do.' Dr B.J. Fogg looked for ways to make the new habit easier to do. Each step of the new habit is for more nuanced changes and look for better ways to do it. Then see what might go wrong or kill you and think about ways to stop this happening.

Leaving the habit of smoking

Something like this can happen (after going through your addiction process and visualizing your higher purpose): you take out a favourite chewing gum from a little pocket with a zipper when you feel the cue for cigarettes.

Then you'll keep the gum in your mouth for 5 seconds and enjoy the minty taste before you start chewing. While doing this, you are going to close your eyes and play your positive quit smoking mental video.

Instead, while keeping your hands folded, you will start chewing slowly to avoid fidgeting. To avoid the situation of not getting a chewing gum, you must ensure that at all times, you have at least one pack in your purse or bag, one at home and one at the office. You are going to check every morning when you get ready to leave home and first thi9ng when you get to the office.

If you are having a smoking craving, you are going to excuse yourself and take a brisk 10-minute walk. Walk to energize yourself before you get back to work.

We make good habits stick when we commit ourselves. Because in everything we do in life, we value our spiritual selves, or don't. We must first find ourselves worthy of more and greater to achieve everything that lies in universal escrow.

So often in life, you introduce to other people your talents and resources. You make others a priority and you abandon yourself for the last time. The problem with this is when the rest of the world is 'pleased,' it's hardly time to look after who's most important, you.

Building good habits requires conscious thinking and planning. Whether it's increased exercise, more religious studies, learning, closer relationships, or perhaps healthier eating, it means setting aside time to decide what we like. We must permit ourselves to go after it when we know what it is.

Very often, we fell into the trap of knowing what we need, so we put it off for the future until 'the time is right.' It's always the right time! There's a saying, 'How it is now!' Make and go to your commitment!

Steps for sticking to habits

1. Be worthy: If you don't believe you're deserving of it, you won't ever manifest what you want out of life. Your worthiness rate is directly proportionate to what you can achieve. Understanding that you are as worthy as anybody else on this planet to accomplish your goals is vital to enter the process fully.

2. Consider your well-being a priority: This does not mean that we are disregarding our obligations. Maybe it's about encouraging others to be more worried about themselves rather than thinking we've got to do it all. There is a fine line in encouraging others to take on real responsibility.

3. Study your area of interest: There's so much data out there, and we can find almost any information we want with Google. We have already started to form your new habit by looking for your target. You're on the way! The acquisition of appropriate, sound information and knowledge about our targets will educate us in our areas of interest to begin to change our perceptions.

4. Be gentle with yourself: Like any significant change in life, we will sometimes slip back into old habits or lose track of our goals until they become a habit. It takes 30-45 days to create a new habit everywhere. Give a grace period to yourself as you work towards your goal. Missing a day, losing, or going off track is all right. We're more likely to stay in the old pattern if we beat ourselves up. Humanity's acceptance and grace will go a long way!

5. Pat on the back for a well-functioning job: Make yourself a cheerleader and motivational speaker. You know precisely what you need to do to keep going. Do not expect to receive praise from the outside world because somehow others appear to be short of what we need to hear because they come from their own projections.

Our life is our own. No one knows better what is going to nurture our souls and improve our lives than we do! Go for the dreams you have. You never know!

10.3 Start living from the more authentic, the more genuine within you

Most of us are worried about how we can better manage our lives by developing and maintaining better habits. However, the issue with the thinking about this is that you believe you can manage your life continuously discipline as the basic motivating principle.

You watch people apply this idea to their lives every only to see them, shortly afterwards, stop doing whatever they decided to do. Diets fail, exercise programs cease, lovers leave, and we go back and forth to the same old, tired arguments.

Why is it not working?

- You never like to be told what to do and
- You should try to apply Band-Aid to an old identity

Personality is the mask and costume you've been wearing since infancy that you donned from the expectations of your parent. You have become something but are not to remain attached to those you used to belong to. It's not that tag that you are. And at a certain time in your life, you begin to feel the difference between your true self and identity although you may not have the insight to see that this is what it is. You think one way, but you see something else.

You find that between what you want and what you think you have to do is conflicted thinking. A crisis makes you realize that you have lived a life that is not true to who you are. These are signals that you're beginning to wake up to who you are. To form behaviour patterns that satisfy you (i.e., good habits), you must start living the more authentic, more genuine you. The authentic self has its urges, desires, and living patterns, and it's all about wholeness. In the beginning, the task of discovering the authentic self is to hear; then live in its messages.

Cognitive-behavioural therapy: how to restructure CBT-related thoughts

Are your brain, thoughts, and habits unhelpful? Knowing this can assist cognitive behavioural therapy. Cognitive behavioural therapy is a form of psychotherapy that addresses problems and boosts happiness by modifying dysfunctional emotions, behaviours, and thoughts. Instead of deconstructing your childhood, cognitive behavioural therapy reconstructs new, adaptive thoughts to help you form useful habits. Such patterns will change your life's way of living, talking, and behaving. Think of CBT as a way to re-connect your brain. You can use CBT to transform unhelpful habits into effective habits.

Changing habits is not an easy task. There are three steps to changing habits:

1) Recognise what you want to improve and reflect on your behaviour. Identify the habit you want to replace with clear specificity and pay attention when it comes to it. This is being aware of it.

2) Focus on your behaviour when it comes to that habit or craving. Focus on bringing your mind to the habit with which you wish to replace it. Remember to focus on why you want to change or the

advantages and disadvantages of acting on the urges. This will give you a very important 'why' to facilitate real change.

3) Purposeful repetition: Repetition is essential for developing new neural pathways in your brain. Stay conscious and purposeful in replacing the old habit with the new habit. Practice this action until it transforms into second nature.

Conclusion

Hacks to Change Habits in Thirty Days

You would only thrive as an early human if you had developed practical behaviours that kept you healthy and prosperous. To this end, your mind/body set new neural tracks automatically for whatever you repeatedly did.

Who would better feed his family: the hunter who stood his bow and arrow every night in the same place, or the one who got up every morning and had to search for them in the cave? Who would encourage her child to survive: the mother who regularly tested to see if she breastfed her baby or the one who did it erratically? Okay, you're getting the picture.

Here are five tips for building useful habits:

Tip #1: Intentionally, when comfortable, develop habits.

Practice specific ways to do something if you're not overwhelmed because, with pressure, people tend to fall back on routines - whether good or bad.

In a recent experiment, psychologist Wendy Wood, Ph.D., of the University of Southern California and one of the world's leading experts in habit formation, found that students fell into autopilot around the time of the test. If you get in the groove when relaxed, then when you are stressed, you are more likely to stay in the groove.

Tip #2: Identify why you don't want a new habit to grow.

People have mixed feelings about developing new behaviours, so be sure to consider what holds you back: time, commitment, motivation, a lack of immediate gratification, cash, and so on. You're not terrible at shifting mental barriers. You're just human.

Tip #3: Practice tolerance for irritation and delay gratification.

Research tells us that people who defer gratification for future happiness (instant pleasure) are better able to tolerate disappointment than those who catch short-term fixes. Stop doing something that is not healthy for you for a minute, or 10 minutes, or an hour, or until tomorrow.

Use thought incrementally. To soothe the disappointment with words of compassion and encouragement, say: I can do this, I'll be okay without my quick fix, and I'll love how I feel like making a healthy choice.

Tip #4: Highlight yourself and be proud of every little step you take to create a new habit.

It doesn't work to blame yourself. It only makes you feel bad and less likely to want to do good things. Reward yourself with generous congratulations when you make a positive choice and make you feel proud. It works better to feel proud than to be shameful.

Tip #5: Make sure you give yourself a new habit, but not to please others.

To make others happy or to stop being shamed by them, most people try to change. Make sure you're doing it for yourself and know why you're going to benefit from the change.

Changing habits is the most challenging thing we all face in our lives as no one is prepared to come out of their comfort zone and change their routine, setting priorities, leaving what you like for what is good for you. Habits are sometimes seen in the form of addictions. By following the above steps, you should be able to change your practices and your habits successfully; but changing or leaving cravings is not as easy as changing your habit to rise early. But it can be easy compared to abstaining from alcohol. Still, if you are motivated and consistent, you can manage to control yourself and leave your harmful habits. Leading a happy and healthy life should be your goal: improvement is life.

For further details: such as coaching and free downloadable resources see our website here: www.mindsetmastership.com

238

References

- Anastacia. (n.d.). The Golden Loop of Habit Change. *https://www.bloomsandsmiles.com/the-golden-loop-of-habit-change/.*

- Barnett, M. (n.d.). Good Habits, Bad Habits: A Conversation with Wendy Wood. *https://behavioralscientist.org/good-habits-bad-habits-a-conversation-with-wendy-wood/.*

- Clear, J. (n.d.). The Ultimate Habit Tracker Guide: Why and How to Track Your Habits. *https://jamesclear.com/habit-tracker.*

- Daniels, E. (n.d.). strategies to stay stick with your new habits. *https://learnevolveandthrive.com/how-to-make-good-habits-stick/.*

- Edblad, P. (n.d.). https://patrikedblad.com/habits/how-to-change-your-habits.

- Intrinsic Motivation. (n.d.). *https://psychology.iresearchnet.com/social-psychology/control/intrinsic-motivation/.*

- K. (n.d.). https://www.lifehack.org/797417/how-to-make-changes-in-life. *How to Make Changes in Life To Be The Best Version of You.*

- Logo, H. (n.d.). How to Change Habits and Start New Ones Using the Habit Loop. *https://habit.com/blog/2018/01/18/change-habits-start-new-ones-using-habit-loop/*

- Maltz., M. (1960). Psycho-Cybernetics.

- Parrish, R. (1992). Disrupting Habitual Patterns Through Meditation. Pp. https://mindworks.org/blog/overcoming-habitual-patterns-meditation/.

- Pei-Ying Lin, W. W. (2015, November 9). Healthy eating habits protect against temptations. *https://dornsife.usc.edu/assets/sites/545/docs/lin.wood.monterosso.2016.pdf.*

- Petsinger, D. K. (n.d.). 6 Signs It's Time to Change Your Life. *https://www.lifehack.org/368124/6-signs-its-time-change-your-life.*

- Stillman, J. (2016, July). This 1 Science-Backed Rule Is All You Need to Stay Motivated. pp. https://www.inc.com/jessica-stillman/follow-this-1-rule-to-maintain-peak-motivation.html.

- Ryder, J. (2014, Jun 22,). https://www.psychologytoday.com/us/blog/hypnosis-the-power-trance/201406/hypnotic-regression-and-healing-the-unconscious-mind.

Printed in Great Britain
by Amazon

20200352R00139